THE NEW YORK PUBLIC LIBRARY AMAZING HISPANIC AMERICAN HISTORY

A Book of Answers for Kids

George Ochoa

A Stonesong Press Book

John Wiley & Sons, Inc.

New York • Chichester • Weinheim • Brisbane • Singapore • Toronto

To my parents, Oswaldo and Misterio Ochoa, born in Ecuador, citizens of the United States.

I would like to thank Paul Fargis, Kerry Acker, and Ellen Scordato of the Stonesong Press, and Kate Bradford of John Wiley & Sons. A special thanks to my wife Melinda Corey and daughter Martha Corey-Ochoa for their love and support.

This book is printed on acid-free paper. ⊗

Copyright ©1998 by The New York Public Library and The Stonesong Press, Inc.
All rights reserved.
Published by John Wiley & Sons, Inc.

Published simultaneously in Canada.

No part of this publication may be reproduced, stored in a retrieval system or transmitted in any form or by any means, electronic, mechanical, photocopying, recording, scanning, or otherwise, except as permitted under Sections 107 or 108 of the 1976 United States Copyright Act, without either the prior written permission of the Publisher, or authorization through payment of the appropriate per-copy fee to the Copyright Clearance Center, 222 Rosewood Drive, Danvers, MA 01923, (978) 750-8400, fax (978) 750-4744. Requests to the Publisher for permission should be addressed to the Permission Department, John Wiley & Sons, Inc., 605 Third Avenue, New York, NY 10158-0012, (212) 850-6011, fax (212) 850-6008, E-Mail: PERMREQ@WILEY.COM.

This publication is designed to provide accurate and authoritative information in regard to the subject matter covered. It is sold with the understanding that the publisher is not engaged in rendering legal, accounting, or other professional services. If legal advice or other expert assistance is required, the services of a competent professional person should be sought.

The name "The New York Public Library" and the representation of the lion appearing in this work are trademarks and the property of The New York Public Library, Astor, Lenox, and Tilden Foundations.

Library of Congress Cataloging-in-Publication Data

Ochoa, George.
    The New York Public Library amazing Hispanic American history: a book of answers for kids / George Ochoa.
        p.   cm. — (New York Public Library answer books for kids series)
    "A Stonesong Press book."
    Includes index.
    Summary: Consists of questions and answers about Latinos revealing the common history which unites them while also showing how they differ depending upon their country of origin.
    ISBN 0-471-19204-X (pbk.: alk. paper)
    1. Hispanic Americans—History—Miscellanea—Juvenile literature.
2. Children's questions and answers [1. Hispanic Americans—Miscellanea. 2. Questions and answers.] I. Title. II. Series.
E184.S75029   1998
973' .0468—dc21   98-23797

Printed in the United States of America

10 9 8 7 6 5 4 3 2 1

CONTENTS

INTRODUCTION

Why do so many California towns have Spanish names? What's the difference between a taco and an enchilada? Are Puerto Ricans foreigners? Why do so many Cuban exiles hate Fidel Castro? Are Hispanics a race?

The number of Hispanic Americans is growing every day. As it does, questions like these grow in number as well. Even someone who is Hispanic often knows little about the heritage of Hispanics from other countries. A Mexican American, for example, may know little about what it is like to come from Colombia. What unites and divides people from places as far-flung as Chile and El Salvador? A good place to look for answers is the New York Public Library, or your own local library. Or you can start with this book.

The New York Public Library Amazing Hispanic American History: A Book of Answers for Kids answers your questions about Latinos—including why many of them prefer to be called Latino, not Hispanic. It answers such basic questions as "Are Latin America and South America the same thing?" (they are not) and "From what countries do most Hispanic Americans come?"It recounts the common history that unites all Hispanic Americans. Country by country, it shows how Mexicans differ from Puerto Ricans, and Cubans from Dominicans. It satisfies your curiosity about every topic from machismo to dancing, and every Latino celebrity from Antonio Banderas to Mariah Carey. Want to know what a bodega or a zoot suit is? Check the glossary at the end.

Whether you know someone who is a Hispanic American, are one yourself, or are just interested in how Latinos are changing your country, this book is for you. We hope it will encourage you to spend time at the library—maybe even the New York Public Library—finding out more. Better still, ask a Hispanic American to tell you about his or her heritage. If this book helps you to understand that person's story—or your own—it will have succeeded.

What is a Hispanic? ◆ How many Hispanic American
ive in the United States? ◆ How many Hispani
Americans are children? ◆ Are Hispanic Americans th
country's la gro ? y not ca
Hispanic Americans "Spanish Americans"? ◆ Are Lati
America an th A e the eth g? ◆ If yo
ask an immigra t o ou eio tell you th
differenc between a taco and an enchilada will she b
able to w E is L in e p ure s
different from place to place? ◆ Are there any similaritie
among Hispanic Americans? ◆ Why do some peopl
call themselves Hispanic while others call themselve

WHO ARE HISPANIC AMERICANS?

What is a Hispanic?

A **Hispanic** is a person who descends from Spanish forebears or from one of the many cultures in the world that owe their origins to Spain. The term comes from *Hispania*, the Latin word for Spain used by the ancient Romans, who conquered that region in the second century B.C. A **Hispanic American** is a Hispanic who is a citizen or resident of the United States.

How many Hispanic Americans live in the United States?

As of 1995, the U.S. Census Bureau counted 26.9 million people of Hispanic origin. This is about 10 percent of the country's total population. In other words, one out of every ten Americans is a Hispanic American.

How many Hispanic Americans are children?

More than 10 million Hispanic Americans are under the age of twenty—about 14 percent of all Americans under twenty. Hispanic Americans are younger on average than American whites, blacks, or Asians. More than 16 percent of kids under five are Hispanic. If you are a young person reading this book, there is a good chance you are a Hispanic American or go to school with someone who is. In the future, your children are even more likely to do so.

Between 1980 and 1990, the Hispanic American community grew by 53 percent—almost five times faster than the rest of the U.S. population.

Are Hispanic Americans the country's largest minority group?

No—African Americans are. But the Census Bureau projects that by the year 2005, Hispanic Americans will surpass African Americans as the country's largest minority group. By the year 2050, Hispanic Americans are expected to account for one-fourth of the U.S. population.

Why not call Hispanic Americans "Spanish Americans"?

Many Hispanics informally call themselves "Spanish," but the term can lead to confusion. Strictly speaking, a Spanish American person is an American whose family comes from Spain. While some Hispanic Americans can claim a direct link to that European nation, most descend from one of the lands in the Americas settled by Spain. Today, most of these lands are part of **Latin America**, which includes such countries as Mexico in North America, El Salvador in Central America, Cuba in the West Indies, and Colombia in South America. Because Spain settled these regions long before the English founded their thirteen American colonies, the history of Latin America stretches back further than that of the United States.

Are Latin America and South America the same thing?

No. South America is a continent connected by the narrow Isthmus of Panama to the separate continent of North America. South America extends from Colombia to Chile. To say "South America" is to talk about a geographical entity.

What do the English words cork, anchovy, alligator, parade, guitar, ranch, vigilante, canyon, *and* filibuster *have in common? They were all borrowed from Spanish.*

Latin America is a cultural entity. South America is part of it, but so are some North American countries: Mexico, the nations of Central America, and some of the islands of the Caribbean Sea. What makes all these places "Latin American" is that their people speak languages derived from Latin. Spanish, spoken in most of Latin America, is a Latin-derived language; so are Portuguese, which is spoken in Brazil, and French, which is spoken in Haiti and Martinique.

If you ask an immigrant from South America to tell you the difference between a taco and an enchilada, will she be able to answer?

Not necessarily. Someone born and raised in the United States will be more likely to know the answer. Mexican dishes like **tacos** and **enchiladas** are better known in the United States than they are to people in many parts of Latin America. Each Latin American country has distinct cuisine and customs. (If you want to know the difference, see the chapter Coming From Mexico.)

From Panama to Argentina

Fly from California to New York, and you are still in the same country. Fly the same distance from Panama to Argentina, and you are in a different world. The two countries are a case study in how different Hispanic cultures can be.

Panama is a tiny tropical nation heavily covered with rain forest. Most of its people are a blend of European and Native American ancestry. Their national dance, the *tamborito*, is rooted in the music of African slaves brought forcibly to the coast centuries ago. Almost all Panamanians are farmers; many harvest bananas. Panama's greatest claim to international fame is the U.S.-built Panama Canal, which runs through the country, linking the Atlantic and Pacific Oceans. To protect its interests in this nearby nation, the United States invaded Panama as recently as 1989. Full control of the canal will be turned over to Panama on January 1, 2000.

Just a short flight away from Antarctica, Argentina is nowhere near the United States and has not been closely connected with it. It is a large country—about one-third the size of the United States—in a temperate climate with snowcapped mountains higher than the Alps. Most of Argentina's population is entirely descended from Europeans. Its capital, Buenos Aires, is an international cultural center. Argentinian authors such as Manuel Puig and Jorge Luis Borges are read throughout the world. Many Argentinians engage in sheep and cattle ranching on wide open plains. The *gaucho*, or cowboy, lives in the national mythology much as Western heroes live in the dreams of North Americans. Argentina's best-known dance is the sophisticated **tango**, now danced in ballrooms worldwide.

Despite their differences, both the Panamanians and the Argentinians speak Spanish, and both are Hispanic.

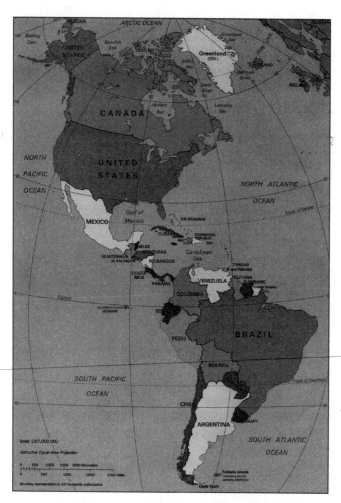

More than twenty-five nations lie south of the United States. Of these, twenty are generally considered part of Latin America, which includes both Spanish-speaking countries and those where Portuguese and French are spoken.

Why is Latin American culture so different from place to place?

Latin America consists of twenty different nations, not to mention several territories of still more nations—including Puerto Rico, a U.S. commonwealth that someday may become the fifty-first state. The English colonies of North America developed into just two countries—the United States and Canada. But Spain's American colonies never united in the same way. They developed from colonial times as separate realms in places of great geographic diversity—Mexican deserts, Amazon jungles, Andean mountains. Once independent of Spain, they stayed stubbornly independent of each other. Over hundreds of years of historical ups and downs, they became vastly different from each other.

Are there any similarities among Hispanic Americans?

There certainly are. Most, though not all, are Roman Catholic. Many believe strongly in the importance of family and community. They share the kind of indebtedness to Spanish culture that Americans have to English culture. For example, they honor Miguel de Cervantes, the Spanish author of *Don Quixote*, much as Americans honor William Shakespeare. Their varied musical styles—from **mariachi** to **salsa**—show the influence of the Native American and African ancestors who are an important part of their ethnic heritage. Many, but not all, are a genetic mix of European and Native American, and sometimes of African as well. For that reason, many, but not all, have "brown" skin as opposed to "white" or "black" skin. Some of their favorite foods share similarities in ingredients and spices. And, of course, they all speak Spanish—or descend from people who did.

On the other hand, there are some supposed commonalities that are not real. Hispanic Americans do not all speak with accents. They do not all work as fruit pickers or housecleaners. They did not all come to this country illegally. These stereotypes are part of the prejudice that Hispanic Americans face every day. The experience of bigotry unites them just as their cultural similarities do. It has made Hispanic Americans more ready than ever to put aside their differences and work together for social and political acceptance and equality of opportunity.

Why do some people call themselves Hispanic while others call themselves Latino?

"Don't call me 'High-Spanic'" proclaims a web site run by a person of Latin American descent. For many who share that ethnicity, the only acceptable term is **Latino** (for men) or **Latina** (for women).

Why should "Hispanic" be insulting? After all, it is used by no less prestigious an agency than the U.S. Census Bureau. But many Latinos consider it an ugly word invented

Throughout U.S. history, thirty-eight Latinos have been awarded the Congressional Medal of Honor, the country's highest military honor.

by English-speakers to talk about aliens. It has a pseudoscientific English word ending: "-ic," as in "metric system" or "sulfuric acid." In contrast, "Latino" is a real Spanish word that Latin Americans use to describe themselves. Left-wing Latinos tend to be especially annoyed by "Hispanic."

However, "Hispanic" has a lot of champions. They argue that "Hispanic," like "Latino," is based on a real Spanish word, **hispano**, which can mean either Hispanic or Spanish. True, the word ending is English, but why shouldn't an English word have an English ending? A German American doesn't usually complain because Americans don't call him "Deutsch."

Some people say "Hispanic" is misleading because it derives from the Latin word for Spain, rather than referring directly to Latin America. But "Latino," in its essence, refers to the Latin language of the Romans who conquered Spain—which has even less to do with Latin America.

Despite the controversy, either term is acceptable in polite speech, and both are used interchangeably in this book.

Is "Chicano" just another word for "Hispanic"?

No. **Chicano** (or "Chicana," for a female) refers only to a Mexican American, an American of Mexican descent. It is an abbreviation of the word *Mexicano*, Spanish for "Mexican." It was originally an insult, a term of disdain used by non-Hispanics. But in the mid-twentieth century, Mexican Americans themselves started saying it with pride. Nowadays, to call oneself a Chicano is to honor one's own Mexican heritage.

What is an Anglo?

Technically, an Anglo American or **Anglo** is an American descended from the Anglo-Saxon peoples of England. But Hispanics use the term more broadly, for any white, English-speaking American not of Hispanic descent.

As of 1990, 25.8 percent of California's population and 25.5 percent of Texas's were Hispanic Americans.

If your parents are Brazilian, are you a Hispanic American?

No. Although it is the largest country in South America, Brazil was colonized by Portugal, not Spain. Most of its people speak Portuguese, not Spanish. The languages are similar enough that a Spanish-speaker can sometimes manage a conversation with a Portuguese-speaker, but they are not the same.

On the other hand, Brazilians are Latin Americans, because they come from a country south of the United States that speaks a Latin-based language. In that sense, you could call a Brazilian a Latino, but not a Hispanic.

Are Hispanics a race?

Not really—but it is hard to tell because race is such a fuzzy word. When someone talks about race, the speaker is distinguishing groups of people based on some standard he or she thinks is important and physically inherited. In the United States, people usually talk about the races as white, black (or African American), Asian, American Indian, and Hispanic. The U.S. Census Bureau accepts all these categories except Hispanic. The bureau notes that "persons of Hispanic origin may be of any race." Why the confusion?

Hispanics really can be of any race, as most Americans would define the term. Many Latin Americans are of mixed racial origin, combining European, Native American, and, sometimes, African stocks. But this mixture varies wildly, making it impossible to assign to Hispanics a uniform

Were They Hispanic?

Singer Carmen Miranda and dancer José Greco were well known for performing "Latin acts"—but neither of them were Hispanic.

Carmen Miranda (1913–1955) was born in Portugal as Maria do Carmo Miranda da Cunha. She grew up in Brazil before becoming a musical star of Broadway and Hollywood. Known as the "Brazilian Bombshell," she played many Latino roles. She was famous for dancing with a bowl of fruit on her head.

José Greco, the master of **flamenco** and other Spanish dances, was born Costanzo Greco in Italy in 1918 and was raised in Brooklyn. From the 1930s onward, he helped popularize Spanish dancing in the United States. On his habit of passing for Hispanic, he said: "After all, when people go to see a Spanish dancer, they like to think he is Spanish."

"A simple definition of the Hispanic could be: a person with a willingness to mix and therefore a person with a disposition to create new types of human relationships and new types of cultural forms, or to develop new perceptions of man and reality. Color to us is an accident, not a definition of the human person."
—Puerto Rican historian, Arturo Morales Carrión

shade of "brown." Many Puerto Ricans are part African. Many Guatemalans are pure Mayan, a Native American people. Some Argentinians are pure Spanish, others pure German or Italian. Peruvian president Alberto Fujimori of Peru is of Japanese descent. To say someone is Hispanic is to say nothing definite about his "race."

If Hispanics are not a race, why are they often thought of as one? People who think this way must feel the difference between them and Hispanics is important enough to call "racial." Some may be uncomfortable with the easy way in which Hispanic nations have historically mixed races. The truth is, with their wide range of skin tones, Hispanics defy the very idea of race as something fixed and absolute.

If Hispanics are not a race, why do they call themselves la raza?

Spanish for "race," the term *la raza* was first popularized by Chicano political activists in the 1960s. Used originally to refer to people of Mexican descent, it is now accepted by many other Hispanic Americans. To be part of *la raza* suggests not so much skin color as unity of origin and purpose, along with a sense of belonging to a common culture.

No Relation

In the 1950s, when José Ferrer and Mel Ferrer were popular movie stars, people often assumed they were related. In fact, their parents didn't even come from the same country.

José Vicente Ferrer de Otero y Cintron (1912–1992) was born in Puerto Rico. He became famous for his stage and film portrayal of the title role in *Cyrano de Bergerac*, and won a Best Actor Oscar for the film version (1950). His other film roles included French painter Toulouse-Lautrec in *Moulin Rouge* (1952). His son Miguel Ferrer, born in 1954, is also an actor, seen in the film *Robocop* (1987) and the TV series "Twin Peaks" and "Lateline."

Mel Ferrer (1917–) was born in New Jersey as Melchior Gaston Ferrer. His father was a Cuban-born surgeon. His films included *Scaramouche* (1952) and *War and Peace* (1956).

Besides being Hispanic Americans, the two Ferrers shared one thing in common: they both attended Princeton University.

From what countries do most Hispanic Americans come?

If you held a party for twenty representative Hispanic Americans, twelve of them would have their roots in Mexico. Two would hail from Puerto Rico, and one would tell you about his or her family in Cuba. The other five would represent a mix of about seventeen other countries, mostly in Central and South America.

To put it another way, more than 60 percent (13.5 million) of the 22.4 million Hispanic Americans counted in 1990 were of Mexican descent. About 12 percent (2.7 million) were Puerto Rican and 4 percent (one million) were Cuban. The rest of the Latino population descends from other Spanish-speaking countries.

Will it still be true fifty years from now that most Hispanic Americans come from Mexico, Puerto Rico, and Cuba?

Maybe not. The face of the Hispanic American community is changing. Many immigrants still come from Mexico but few from Cuba. Puerto Ricans migrate to the United States in smaller numbers than they did in the 1950s and 1960s. However, immigration from the Dominican Republic has ballooned in the past few decades. So has immigration from such Central American nations as El Salvador, Guatemala, and Nicaragua, and such South American nations as Colombia, Ecuador, and Peru.

Are all Hispanic Americans immigrants?

No, but many of them are. According to 1995 Census Bureau figures, about 39 percent of Hispanic Americans were born in a foreign country. They account for 46 percent—nearly half—of the 23 million foreign-born people in the United States. Not surprisingly, Spanish is the language other than English that is most commonly spoken in the United States.

Do all Hispanic Americans speak Spanish as their first language?

No, but it is a common myth that they do. Studies show that Mexican Americans whose families have been in the

In order, the three U.S. metropolitan areas with the largest numbers of Hispanic Americans are Los Angeles, New York, and Miami–Fort Lauderdale.

An exuberant young crowd at the Dominican Day parade in New York, New York, celebrates their Hispanic heritage.

United States for three generations speak little if any Spanish. As with other ethnic groups, Hispanic immigrants learn as much English as they need to, but often feel more comfortable using their native language in private. However, their American-born children typically speak English first, Spanish second. Distant descendants may speak no Spanish at all.

Why, then, is so much Spanish spoken in California, Texas, Florida, New York, and other favorite destinations for Hispanic Americans? One reason is that so many Hispanic Americans are recent immigrants. Fifty years from now, their descendants will be speaking English, and maybe nothing more.

But many children of Hispanic immigrants are not so eager to forget their parents' language. Family-oriented and community-minded, they like being able to speak in Spanish with their parents, relatives, and the many newly arriving Latinos in other parts of town. Hispanic Americans often visit their ancestral countries, a practice that helps them keep alive their cultural loyalty and Spanish proficiency. For all these reasons, Spanish may long be spoken among Hispanic Americans in a way that has rarely occurred among ethnic groups of previous times.

Why do so many Hispanic Americans come from Mexico, Puerto Rico, and Cuba?

Mexico is just over the border from Texas and the American Southwest. Cross a river or step over a line in the desert, and you've switched countries. Immigration laws limit how many Mexicans can enter legally—but many enter illegally.

Puerto Rico is part of the United States. Puerto Ricans are U.S. citizens by birth. Going from the island of Puerto Rico to the North American mainland is as easy as flying north.

The island of Cuba is closer to the United States than Puerto Rico. It has been ruled by communist dictator Fidel Castro since 1959. The United States has long been anticommunist and anti-Castro. People fleeing Castro's Cuba have therefore been welcomed as political refugees.

Why don't Hispanic Americans come from the island of Jamaica?

The island of Jamaica is nearly as close to the United States as Cuba, but it isn't Hispanic. Its people speak English, not Spanish.

Why do Cubans speak Spanish, but not Jamaicans? Why does the United States own Puerto Rico but not Mexico? Come to think of it, if Spain got to the Americas before the English, why don't all Americans speak Spanish?

These questions can only be answered by looking at history: the history of Spanish explorers and conquerors,

Latin American rebels, American empire builders, and Hispanic Americans. The next chapter, Spanish America, will begin to explain the complex and fascinating history of the Spanish in North and South America. The chapters that follow it will explore the stories and heritage of Latin and Hispanic Americans in depth.

Was Christopher Columbus Spanish? ♦ What was th
first place in the Americas that Columbus landed?
Are the Bahamas still owned by Spain? ♦ Where in th
Americas did the Spanish first settle? ♦ Did Columbu
ever set foot in what is now the mainland United States
♦ What became of Columbus's first settlement, L
Navidad? ♦ Who were the Native Americans o
Hispaniola? ♦ What became of the Arawak? ♦ Whe
did the Spanish start conquering the mainland part o
the Americas? ♦ How did Montezuma lose his empire
♦ Why was Mexico valuable to Spain? ♦ What di
the Spanish do about the Aztec religion? ♦ Wha

SPANISH AMERICA

Was Christopher Columbus Spanish?

No. The explorer who first visited the Americas on October 12, 1492, was Italian, but he was working for Spain. Born in Genoa, Italy, Christopher Columbus (1451–1506) had convinced the Spanish monarchs Ferdinand and Isabella that he could find a route to Asia by sailing west across the Atlantic Ocean. His three ships had Spanish names (the *Niña*, *Pinta*, and *Santa Maria*), sailed Spanish flags, and were crewed by Spanish sailors.

Known in Spanish as Cristóbal Colón, Columbus is considered a virtual native son to Latinos. Columbus Day, the day commemorating his discovery, is celebrated by many Hispanic Americans as *El Día de la Raza*, the "Day of the Race." The holiday is so named because Columbus's coming to America marked the birth of the Latin American people— a mix of European, Native American, and African lineages.

What was the first place in the Americas that Columbus landed?

People today flock to the Bahamas, an island group in the West Indies, for fun and relaxation on its sunny beaches. Columbus was happy just to find dry land there. His crew came ashore on a Bahamian island known to its natives as Guanahaní. Columbus renamed it San Salvador and claimed it for Spain.

The first of Columbus's crew to spot the New World was a Latino: Rodrigo de Triana, the Spanish lookout on the Pinta.

Are the Bahamas still owned by Spain?

Columbus began his New World adventures in the Bahamas, but the Spanish never settled on the islands. It was the English who founded the first European colonies there in the mid-seventeenth century. The islands of the Bahamas remained a British colony until independence was granted in 1973.

Where in the Americas did the Spanish first settle?

On his first voyage, Columbus discovered both Cuba and Hispaniola, two of the four large West Indian islands known as the Greater Antilles. (The other two are Jamaica and Puerto Rico.) His first colony was founded on Hispaniola, an island that today is divided into the Dominican Republic and Haiti. The island's name stems from *Española*, "Spanish Lady."

Columbus decided to found a settlement on Hispaniola because of what he considered an act of God. On Christmas Day, his flagship, the *Santa Maria*, ran aground on a reef off

Discovered What?

We talk about Christopher Columbus discovering the Americas, as though no one had ever seen them before. But of course, millions of people had—the Native Americans who already lived here. By at least 12,000 years ago, the ancestors of modern Native Americans had already migrated from Asia to America. By the time of Columbus, they were living throughout the Western Hemisphere.

Around 1000 A.D., a Norse mariner named Leif Eriksson became the first European known to visit the Americas. He found an area he called Vinland, believed by some experts to have been in present-day Newfoundland. Vinland had been forgotten by the time of Columbus.

From a European point of view, Columbus really did discover America. That is, until he saw and reported the existence of this land, Europeans had no permanent knowledge of it. Once Columbus told them, Europeans never forgot.

In this book, we talk about Columbus and other European explorers "discovering" places in the Americas. This is true, from a European point of view. From a Native American point of view, it was the Native Americans who discovered Columbus in 1492.

A 1493 illustration depicts Columbus setting off for the New World. This picture accompanied a letter Columbus sent to Sanchez, one of his many correspondents.

the island. Instead of being discouraged, Columbus took it as a sign that God wanted him to start a colony. The island was an attractive place to settle: a warm, well-watered land of lushly forested mountains. He used the ship's wreckage to build a makeshift fort that he called La Navidad, or "Christmas." In January, he set sail for Spain, leaving thirty-nine men at the fort.

Did Columbus ever set foot in what is now the mainland United States?

No. That honor awaited other discoverers (see the chapter Before the United States). However, on his second voyage (1493–1496), Columbus did set foot in Puerto Rico, which later became a possession of the United States. He explored many other places in the Americas, including, on the second voyage, Jamaica and the Leeward Islands. On his third voyage (1498–1500), Columbus sailed to Trinidad in the West Indies and Venezuela in South America. On his fourth and last voyage (1502–1504), he reached Honduras in Central America.

What became of Columbus's first settlement, La Navidad?

It did not last long. In 1493, after returning to Hispaniola on his second voyage, Columbus discovered that the little fort had been destroyed. The Spaniards at the fort had abused the local Native Americans, taking slaves and raping women. The locals responded by killing the invaders and destroying their settlement.

Having brought with him a much larger group of 1,500 men, Columbus founded new and bigger colonies on the island, Isabella and Santo Domingo. The latter is today the capital of the Dominican Republic and the oldest surviving European city in the Americas. The new colonists proceeded to treat the local Native Americans much the same as La Navidad's settlers had.

Who were the Native Americans of Hispaniola?

They were Arawak, members of a Native American language group still found in South America. They were sometimes known as the Taino; the Ciboney were a related people. At the time of Columbus, Arawak tribes lived in the Bahamas and throughout the Greater Antilles. The Arawak of the West Indies were farmers and fishers. Spanish discoverers described them as generous, handsome people of great hospitality, slow to use their cane spears. Unfortunately for them, some of them wore ornaments of gold.

The Spanish had a burning desire for gold, which in Europe was a currency that could buy anything—banquets, castles, armies. To the Arawak, it was just a decorative metal. The Spanish also wanted slaves, and saw nothing wrong in enslaving the Arawak. In those days, most Christian Europeans felt no strong need to treat non-Christians as human—particularly when they were considered "savages" because of their premodern ways of living.

What became of the Arawak?

Convinced that vast reserves of gold lay somewhere on Hispaniola, Columbus and his settlers set the Arawak to work searching for the yellow ore. Little more than gold dust in streams could be found. Unwilling to go away empty-handed, the Spaniards shipped some Arawak back to Spain as slaves and forced others to work on plantations. Working conditions were terrible. Murder and mutilation were routine punishments. Rebellion was futile; the Spanish were armed with muskets and swords. Many Arawak killed themselves to escape slavery; others died of overwork or diseases brought by the Spanish. By 1550, the Hispaniola Arawak population had been almost entirely wiped out.

Though most of the Caribes of the West Indies were wiped out, about five hundred of these Native Americans still live on a reservation on the island of Dominica.

Were Native Americans treated differently in other parts of the West Indies?

Elsewhere in the West Indies, the Arawak were exterminated just as they were on Hispaniola. So were the Caribes, the Native American people who gave their name to the Caribbean Sea. It is estimated that the Native Americans of the West Indies numbered 6 million in 1492. After two centuries of Spanish and, later, English colonization, they were virtually extinct. A few individuals survived, but as they intermarried with Europeans and Africans, they lost their original way of life.

Why did Columbus call Native Americans "Indians"?

He called them indios, or "Indians," because he felt sure that he had reached the Indies, the region we now call

Proving Columbus Right

Columbus's geography was wrong, but his basic idea was right. It was possible to reach Asia by sailing west from Spain. Portuguese navigator Ferdinand Magellan (c. 1480–1521) provided the proof with his final expedition.

Working for the Spanish crown, Magellan set sail from Spain in 1519. His fleet traveled to the southern tip of South America, through the strait now named the Strait of Magellan. From there the expedition traveled to Indonesia, around the southern tip of Africa, and, in 1522, back to Spain.

The expedition was the first to circumnavigate, or circle, the globe. Only one of the five original ships finished the trip, and only 18 of the original crew of 266. Magellan was not one of them. He was killed in a fight with natives in the Philippines in 1521. Yet he thought of and led the expedition, and is given credit for its success.

Asia. That is why the islands he explored are known to this day as the West Indies. Columbus never wanted to discover a New World: just to find a fast sea route to the rich trading ports of China, India, and Indonesia. He did not realize that Asia lay thousands of miles away, across the Pacific Ocean. As far as he knew at his death in 1506, he died a failure.

What did the Spanish do in the Americas after Columbus died?

Columbus had not found a sea route to Asia, but the Spanish were not disappointed. Not long after Columbus died in 1506, they began to realize that this New World, as they called it, was valuable in its own right. They called it America, after an Italian navigator named Amerigo Vespucci who claimed he was the real discoverer of the American mainland. He is believed to have explored South America in 1499–1500.

Though gold could not be found in large quantities in the West Indies, the islands had other resources. They had fertile soil for raising cattle and planting sugar. Soon after Columbus's death, several enterprising and ruthless Spanish adventurers, known to history by the Spanish term "conquistadors," set out to conquer the lands near Hispaniola.

When did Cuba and Puerto Rico become Spanish?

Two men who had sailed with Columbus conquered these islands soon after Columbus's death. In 1511, Spanish soldier Diego de Velázquez (c. 1465–c. 1524) began his conquest of Cuba by founding Baracoa, the first Spanish colony on the island. Appointed governor of Cuba, he founded Havana, the present-day capital of Cuba, in 1514.

Beginning in 1508, Juan Ponce de León (c. 1460–1521) conquered the island he named Puerto Rico, Spanish for "rich port." He governed it from 1509 to 1512 and founded a settlement called Caparra (1511). The settlement was relocated and renamed San Juan, the present-day capital, in 1521.

Jamaica, another West Indian island, was conquered by the Spanish in 1509. Its capital, Santiago de la Vega (now Spanish Town), was founded about 1525. Jamaica's current capital is Kingston.

Wherever the Spanish went in the West Indies, they enslaved the local Native Americans, just as they had in Hispaniola. Slavery led quickly to extermination. In Puerto Rico, for example, Ponce de León shot six thousand Arawak for rebelling against his harsh rule. An epidemic of smallpox, a disease imported from the Old World, wiped out most of the rest.

If Jamaica was settled by the Spanish, why do people there speak English?

What language people speak in the West Indies has to do with who was the final winner in colonizing their land. The same holds true on the American mainland. That is why people in the United States, a former British colony, speak English.

Spain was all alone at first in the game of colonizing America, but it did not stay lonely for long. By the seventeenth century, the English, French, and Dutch were all staking out American colonies of their own. The West Indies, with their fertile soil, good harbors, and strategic closeness to the mainland, were a desirable property. Jamaica was captured by the English in 1655 and formally ceded to England in 1670. (It is now an independent country.) Part of Hispaniola was ceded to France in 1697. That part is now the independent country of Haiti, where French is still spoken.

Who did the Spanish use for workers once the Arawak died out?

It did not occur to the Spanish conquistadors to do the hard work of mining and farming themselves. They wanted to get rich from someone else's labor. At that time, the Portuguese were trading captured Africans as slaves. As the Arawak began to die out, African slaves were shipped in to replace them. The Africans were treated just as brutally, but survived and grew in numbers. Many people of the present-day West Indies are descended, at least in part, from Africans transported there in chains.

When did the Spanish start conquering the mainland part of the Americas?

Cuba and Puerto Rico were nice islands, but the Spanish had greater things in mind. They wanted a vast hoard of treasure—especially gold. They found it in Mexico.

In 1519, Spanish conquistador Hernán Cortés (1485–1547) sailed to Mexico, where he came upon a civilization grander than any yet seen in the New World. The Aztecs, or Mexicas, had dominated Mexico since the fourteenth century. By the time of Cortés, they ruled over a society of millions. The capital city, Tenochtitlán (now Mexico City), was built on an island. Causeways linked it to the mainland, and canals and aqueducts watered it. Impressive pyramids honored the Aztec gods.

Aztec astronomers studied the stars. Artists made sculptures and recorded history in pictographs, or picture writing. Large numbers of commoners served a small ruling class. Captives, especially prisoners of war, were sacrificed regularly to the gods.

By 1521, Cortés had conquered the Aztec civilization. He did it by superior arms and by playing rival groups of Native Americans against each other—especially against their emperor, Montezuma (or Moctezuma) II (c. 1466–1520).

How did Montezuma lose his empire?

Montezuma believed that Cortés was the incarnation of the god-ruler Quetzalcoatl. This deity was usually depicted as a feathered serpent, but a prophecy had said that he would come in the form of a light-skinned, bearded man, and Cortés fit that description. Seeing no point in resisting a god, Montezuma showered Cortés with gifts. Cortés thanked him by taking him prisoner, and tried briefly to rule through him.

The Aztec people rose against Montezuma and the Spanish in 1520. The emperor died in the fighting. Cortés was forced to retreat from Tenochtitlán, but came back with a vengeance the following year. He captured the capital and defeated the empire.

The marines sing "From the halls of Montezuma..." because they occupied the "halls," or palace, of the Aztec emperor in 1847, when the United States conquered Mexico City in the Mexican War.

This Aztec calendar stone is a complicated representation of all of time, from the world's beginning to its end. In the center is the Sun God, surrounded by jaguars, wind, fire, and flood, which the Aztecs believed had ended the four earlier stages of the world. A band of twenty rectangles surrounds these symbols, and represents the twenty days of the thirteen Aztec months. Numerous other symbols represent north, east, west, and south; precious stones; and other elements of the world and time.

Why was Mexico valuable to Spain?

Gold and silver abounded in Mexico. The country also had rich farmlands that were soon put to use growing tobacco, coffee, and sugarcane. These crops could be sold in Europe for a handsome profit.

As in the West Indies, the Spanish wanted someone to do heavy work. But in Mexico, unlike in the West Indies, they found a well-organized people already accustomed to hard labor under an imperial power. The Spanish took the place of the Aztec ruling class, and left almost everything but the people's religion the same. The wealth that had gone to Montezuma now went to them.

What did the Spanish do about the Aztec religion?

The Spanish were fervent Catholics who felt that any other religion was not only wrong but satanic. They had only to look at the Aztec practice of human sacrifice to be convinced that the Aztec religion was devilish indeed. They had little sympathy for the everyday peaceful devotion of the common people to gods such as Tlaloc, who governed rain, or Coyolxauhqui, who ruled the moon.

Our Lady of Guadalupe, the patron saint of Mexico, is a symbol of the nation's blend of Catholicism and Native American traditions. This apparition of the Virgin Mary, the mother of Jesus, came in visions to a Native American, Juan Diego, in 1531. Her feast day, December 12, is honored by many Mexican Americans.

The Spanish made it their business to wipe out the Aztec religion—just as they had done with rival religions at home. Spanish missionaries smashed Aztec idols and preached the Christian Gospel. Yet the Aztec religion never completely disappeared. Some of the people's ancient beliefs and customs were blended into the Mexican version of Roman Catholicism. Aztecs even hid figurines of their deities inside statues of Roman Catholic saints.

What religions were rivals of Catholicism in Spain?

From 711 until 1492, parts of Spain had been ruled by Moors from North Africa, who were Muslims, or believers in Islam. Many Jews lived in Spain as well. In 1492—the same year that Columbus discovered America—the Spanish monarchs Ferdinand and Isabella conquered Granada, the last stronghold of the Moors in Spain. The monarchs considered their victory not only a political one but a mark of God's favor for Catholic Christianity over Islam.

Even before 1492, Jews and Muslims had been subject to persecution and forced conversions. Those who converted were often suspected of secretly practicing their original faiths. The infamous Spanish Inquisition was founded in 1478 mainly as a tool to uncover such closet heretics. Torture was freely used as a means of extracting confessions. Death by burning was a favorite punishment.

It might seem that things could not get worse for Spanish Jews and Muslims, but they did. In 1492, all Jews were forced to leave Spain. The Moors were finally expelled in 1609.

In the Middle Ages, the Moors transformed the Spanish city of Córdoba into a center of culture and learning, known for its great mosque, or Muslim house of worship. When the Spanish reconquered the city in the thirteenth century, they turned the mosque into a Christian cathedral.

Where did the Jews who were expelled from Spain go?

Some went to the Middle East, some to the Netherlands. Many went to the Americas. **Sephardic Jews**, as Jews from Spain and Portugal were known, were an important part of many colonies—particularly Dutch colonies, which tolerated their religion. By the eighteenth century, half of the Europeans in the Dutch colony of Suriname in South America were Jewish.

Conversos, Jews who had converted to Christianity, were an important part of many Spanish colonies. Valued for their expertise in trading and finance, some prospered in the New World. However, they were constantly in danger of being accused of secretly practicing Judaism. Cortés's bookkeeper, a *converso* named Alonso de Avila, reached the high position of mayor of the New Spanish city of Veracruz. He was arrested by the Mexican Inquisition on the trumped-up charge of stepping on a crucifix under his desk.

Did Cortés become the new emperor of Mexico?

He might have wanted to become an emperor, but Spain already had one. Holy Roman Emperor Charles V, who was king of Spain from 1516 to 1556, wanted to keep tight control over any Spanish colonies. He carefully kept Cortés from acquiring any real power over the lands he had conquered.

Instead, in 1535, Charles made Mexico a viceroyalty called New Spain. He named Antonio de Mendoza (c. 1490–1552) as the first viceroy, or royal governor. Under Mendoza and subsequent viceroys, the government and economy of Mexico was organized by **encomiendas**. These grants gave a few Spanish settlers large tracts of land, with jurisdiction over any Native Americans who lived there. Treated little better than slaves, Native Americans were required to pay tribute to the Spanish.

Did anyone object to the treatment of Native Americans?

A few did. Spanish missionary and historian Bartolemé de Las Casas (1474–1566) publicized the atrocities of the con-

The Blood Is Calling

Some Spanish Jews who were forced to convert to Christianity actually did continue to practice Judaism in private. In other cases, families lost all memory of their Jewish roots. Only in modern times has there been a movement in Latin America among people who think they may come from Jewish stock and want to reclaim their heritage. The movement is known in Spanish as *la sangre llama*, or "the blood is calling."

quistadors. He urged that Native Americans be treated humanely and that forced labor be abolished. In 1542, he succeeded in getting the New Laws passed, which aimed to end the *encomienda* system. In fact, very little changed. Forced labor under other names—such as *repartimiento*, or assessment—kept Native Americans working under coercion.

Why were Spanish colonists more prone to mix with Native Americans than English colonists were?

Unlike the English colonists, who usually arrived as families, most of the Spanish conquistadors came to the New World without women. Rather than send back to Spain for wives, they took Native American women to bear their children. The racially mixed children became a new group, called mestizos. In many Latin American countries today, mestizos are a large part of the population. When African slaves were brought to Latin America, the Africans intermarried with other racial groups, adding another element to the mix.

The willingness of Spanish colonists to mix races is in part due to the culture of Spain itself. Located on the Iberian Peninsula in southwest Europe, Spain has been settled and invaded many times. Some invaders, such as the Moors, have come from Africa: at the Strait of Gibraltar, Spain is separated from North Africa by fewer than twenty-five miles of water. As a result of this history, a Spanish person at the time of Columbus was likely to be a blend of cultural influences and ethnic backgrounds—Iberian, Basque, Phoenician, Celt, Italian, Visigoth, Jew, Moor.

The English, in the isolated British Isles, had a far more limited tradition of ethnic mixing: pretty much just Celts and Germanic peoples. The idea of mixing races tended to shock the English in a way that it never shocked the Spanish.

What is the difference between a mestizo and a mulatto?

From the Spanish word for "mixture," a **mestizo** is a person who is a racial mix of European and Native American. A **mulatto** (from an Arabic word for "mixed race") is a person of mixed European and African ancestry. There were mestizos and mulattoes in the English colonies, but many more in the Spanish colonies.

Did the Spanish discriminate among racial groupings?

Discrimination existed in Spanish America, though it varied in degree from colony to colony. In general, the highest privileges and official positions went to pure Spanish people born in Spain. Next down on the ladder of status were **criollos**, or **Creoles**, people born in America of pure Spanish descent. Mestizos and mulattoes stood below them, and pure Native Americans and pure Africans were at the bottom.

When did Mexico get its first printing press?

The first printing press in the New World was installed in Mexico City in 1535. It was one sign of how the colony was developing into a center of urban culture. Churches and palaces were built. A university was founded in Mexico City in 1551. Another university was founded the same year in another part of the Spanish American empire—Lima, Peru.

When did Peru become a Spanish colony?

Conquistador Francisco Pizarro (c. 1475–1541) conquered Peru in 1532–1535. Like Cortés, he did so by destroying a civilization, that of the Incas. Since their civilization was founded about 1200, the Incas had built an empire that spread over two thousand miles, including present-day Ecuador, Peru, Bolivia, and Chile. The empire stretched like a long snake through the Andes Mountains region on the west coast of South America.

Like the Aztecs in Mexico, the Incas had impressive cities, highly developed art, and a religion of many gods. At the top of their highly centralized society was the emperor Atahualpa. Pizarro treacherously captured and murdered him. With horses and firearms (both unknown to the Incas), Pizarro conquered the Inca capital of Cuzco in 1533. He founded a new capital, Lima, in 1535. Peru was made a viceroyalty in 1542.

After conquering Peru, Francisco Pizarro presented himself before Emperor Charles V of Spain. Under Charles V, Spain's empire in the New World expanded greatly.

The *encomienda* system of governing native laborers was put in place in Peru as in Mexico. Missionaries converted the people to Catholicism. The gold and silver of the Incas, like that of the Aztecs, was shipped back to Spain in great quantities.

Do lima beans have anything to do with Lima, Peru?

Lima beans, which are also called butter beans, are named for the city. Cultivated in Peru since prehistoric times, they have been found in ancient graves there. They are only one of many foods that Native Americans cultivated and passed on to Europeans. Others include the tomato, potato, maize (which Americans call corn), chocolate, and many kinds of beans—including lima, kidney, and string beans. Along with these nourishing agricultural products, the New World also gave Europe an

Are These Foods Latin American?

Bananas from Ecuador. Sugar from Cuba. Coffee from Colombia. These foods are so strongly associated with Latin America that many people think they must have originated there. They didn't.

Bananas and sugarcane are both native to tropical Asia. Because they only grow in a warm climate, they flourished when transplanted to the tropical colonies of Latin America. Coffee was first an Arab drink before becoming popular in Europe in the seventeenth century. In 1714, the French managed to transplant a coffee tree to Martinique in the West Indies. Before long, coffee was being grown throughout Latin America, which now produces two-thirds of the world's supply of coffee.

unhealthy one—tobacco. The practice of smoking tobacco spread from the American colonies to Spain and Portugal in the mid-sixteenth century. It gradually became a worldwide habit.

The traffic in agricultural goods went in both directions. The Spanish introduced to the New World such familiar crops as wheat, oats, onions, apples, and oranges. Livestock imported to America by the Spanish included horses, cattle, sheep, and pigs.

How did the rest of South America become Spanish?

As wealth started pouring in from the Americas, the Spanish tried to grab as much of the Western Hemisphere as they could. Venezuela and Colombia, the northernmost countries of South America, were first colonized in the 1520s. The most powerful native American group in the region, the Chibcha of Colombia, was conquered in 1536–1541 by Spanish conquistador Gonzalo Jiménez de Quesada (1495–1579). With the neighboring areas of present-day Ecuador and Panama, Venezuela and Colombia became the colony of New Granada. At first attached to Peru, New Granada became a separate viceroyalty in 1717.

The Spanish conquest of what is now Argentina, in the southern half of South America, began with the founding of Buenos Aires in 1536. In 1776, the viceroyalty of La Plata was established, which included Argentina and the neigh-

Rivers link the port of Buenos Aires, Argentina, to Uruguay, Paraguay, and Brazil. So important is the port, with its bustling trade, that the people of Buenos Aires have historically called themselves porteños, *"people of the port."*

boring lands that now constitute Paraguay, Uruguay, and Bolivia.

Did the penal colony of Devil's Island belong to Spain?

The rocky tropical island where prisoners suffered untold miseries was located off the northeast coast of South America. But it did not belong to Spain. Founded in 1852, it was part of French Guiana. This French colony was part of a small strip of land settled by the Dutch, French, and English rather than the Spanish.

Today, the political entities in this region are named Guyana, Suriname, and French Guiana. English is spoken in the former British colony of Guyana, Dutch in the former Dutch colony of Suriname. Both countries are now independent. French Guiana is a French overseas department, or province.

The biggest non-Spanish part of South America is Brazil, which occupies nearly half the continent of South America.

Why didn't Brazil become Spanish?

In January 1500, Spanish explorer Vicente Yañez Pinzón (c. 1460–c. 1523) became the first known European to reach Brazil. By doing so, he beat Portuguese explorer Pedro Alvares Cabral (c. 1468–1520), who did not make it to Brazil until April. Despite winning the race of discovery, Spain did not lay claim to Brazil.

Spain was held up by a piece of paper called the Treaty of Tordesillas. This 1494 agreement said that all newly discovered lands west of a certain "line of demarcation" would belong to Spain. All lands to the east would belong to Portugal. Brazil lay to the east, and so it became Portuguese. The colony gained independence from Portugal in 1822, but Portuguese, not Spanish, is still the national language.

When did the Spanish conquer Central America?

Brazil is nearly as large in area as the United States, with a population of more than 160 million people.

They did so around the same time they were conquering South America. Spanish conquistador Vasco Nuñez de Balboa (1475–1519) founded the first lasting Spanish colony in Central America at Darien, in what is now Panama, in 1510. Later that century, the Spanish pushed north from Panama and south from Mexico. They conquered most of Central America, the heavily forested tropical region that links North and South America. The Spanish colonies in Central America became the basis for the modern countries of Guatemala, El Salvador, Honduras, Nicaragua, Costa Rica, and Panama—but not Belize.

What was special about Belize?

This tiny country on Central America's east coast was founded by English buccaneers in the early seventeenth century. These pirates lurked on its cays, or small islands, waiting to pounce on Spanish ships bearing gold and silver bound for Spain. Britain kept possession of Belize until 1981, when the colony became independent. English is still the official language.

Belize was not the only haven for pirates. Tortuga, an island near Hispaniola, and Jamaica were also used as bases to raid Spanish ships and colonies at various times until the eighteenth century.

Did Balboa give the Pacific Ocean its name?

Spanish conquistador Vasco Nuñez de Balboa is credited with the European discovery of the Pacific Ocean, but he didn't give it its name. In 1513, guided by Native Americans, he crossed Panama at a point where the isthmus is only forty-five miles from sea to sea. On September 25, he laid eyes for the first time on the glittering vastness of the Pacific Ocean. He claimed this ocean and all the shores it washed for Spain. His name for it was *Mar del Sur*, the "Southern Sea." It was Magellan in 1520 who named it the Pacific, or "peaceful," Ocean.

Who lived in Central America before the Spanish?

Central America and southern Mexico were inhabited from ancient times by several Native American peoples, most notably the Maya. The Maya had a long history of advanced civilization. They developed their own forms of writing, mathematics, and astronomy. They carved cities and farms out of jungle wilderness. In the classic Mayan

"Buccaneer," a common term for a pirate of the West Indies, comes from the French word boucanier. A boucanier was a person from Hispaniola or Tortuga who smoked meat on a boucan, or barbecue frame— perhaps to provide a meal between raids on Spanish ships.

period, from 300 to 900, they built pyramid temples dedicated to their gods.

Long before the Spanish arrived, the classic Mayan civilization mysteriously collapsed. The great cities were left in ruins, to await rediscovery in future centuries. By the 1500s, most Mayans lived in small villages in the Central American forests. They became subjects of the Spanish. However, the Spanish could not get as much profit out of their labor as they could from Mexicans or Peruvians. The hot climate was too harsh, the mineral resources poor. Many Mayans were left more or less untroubled by the Spanish. Remnants of their ancient language, customs, and religion survive to this day.

Why did the Spanish stay in the southern Americas instead of coming north of Mexico?

They did come north of Mexico. The Spanish colonized much of what is now the United States long before the English got there. The next chapter tells the story of that colonization.

here is the present-day border between the Unite
tates and Mexico? ◆ What was the first part of th
present-day United States that the Spanish claimed
◆ Was there rea**B**up**E**o**F**d t**O**be**R**"**E**untain of Youth
n Florida? ◆ W**T**is**H**e**E**ple s**l**iv**n**g town founde
by Europeans in the mainland United States? ◆ Wh
was Florida important to the Spanish? ◆ Who was th
irst E**U**ro**N**e**I**n**T**o**E**ee**D** Ameri**S**an**T**uf**A**a**T**o**E**o**S**ison?
Wh**l**Sp**a**ish ex**l**lo**r**r**s**cov**r**d**t**he**s**ssi**i**p**i**ve
◆ Did de Soto also discover the Grand Canyon?
Who were the Native Americans found by Coronado
diff erently in other parts of the West Indies? ◆ Is "Ch

BEFORE THE UNITED STATES

Where is the present-day border between the United States and Mexico?

The border between Texas and Mexico follows the course of the Rio Grande, or "Big River." West of Texas, the border is an artificial line drawn in the deserts of New Mexico, Arizona, and California. To Spanish conquistadors, the border did not exist. They felt entitled to as much land as they could explore and settle. Probing north from the West Indies and Mexico, they laid claim to much of what is now the United States. Had they kept it all, the official language in many parts of the country would today be Spanish.

What was the first part of the present-day United States that the Spanish claimed?

Florida. Now a favorite spot for vacationers and retirees, this region was claimed for Spain in 1513. The discoverer was Juan Ponce de León, conqueror of Puerto Rico. Discovering it in the Easter season, he named it for *Pascua Florida*, "Floral Passover," a common Spanish name for Easter Sunday. He thought it was an island. Only later did the Spanish realize that it was part of the North American mainland.

First off the Boat

Who first settled the land that is now the United States? The Pilgrims of New England and John Smith of Jamestown get all the publicity. But the Spanish were the first Europeans to set foot in almost half of the nation's states—24 out of 50! The states included the following:

Alabama

Alaska (not counting the Russians, whose country straddles Europe and Asia and who approached from Asia)

Arizona
Arkansas
California
Colorado
Florida
Georgia
Hawaii
Kansas
Louisiana
Mississippi
Nebraska
Nevada

North Carolina
Oklahoma
Oregon
South Carolina
Tennessee
Texas
Utah
Virginia
Washington

In 1526, Spanish explorer Lucas Vázquez de Ayllón (c. 1475–1526) founded a colony in what is now North or South Carolina. It did not long survive its founder's death from fever that year. But it was the first known attempt at European settlement in what is now the United States.

Was there really supposed to be a "Fountain of Youth" in Florida?

Yes. Both Eurasian and Native American legends told of a spring or river that could restore youth and vitality to aging conquistadors. Since Ponce was in his fifties, this sounded pretty good. He landed in Florida near present-day Daytona Beach and searched high and low for the magic waters, but they were never found.

The Fountain of Youth was just one of several mythical American places that lured European explorers to new discoveries. Another was the golden kingdom of El Dorado, falsely rumored to lie somewhere in South America.

What is the oldest surviving town founded by Europeans in the mainland United States?

It is Saint Augustine, Florida, settled in 1565. The founder was Spanish colonizer Pedro Menéndez de Avilés (1519–1574), who brought five hundred colonists with him. The city contains the oldest public square and oldest church in the United States.

Off the mainland, the United States owns an even older city: San Juan, Puerto Rico, whose origins go back to 1511.

Why was Florida important to the Spanish?

Florida had no gold or silver, and the Spanish did not find its soil good for farming. But it had strategic importance: Spanish ships carried treasure home to Spain through the Straits of Florida. Spain felt that it had to hold the colony to protect its sea lanes. In fact, the founder of Saint Augustine was sent there to combat attempted French advances on Florida.

Who was the first European to see American buffalo, or bison?

It was probably Spanish explorer Alvar Núñez Cabeza de Vaca (c. 1490–c. 1560), who survived one of the most incredible adventures any Spaniard underwent.

Cabeza de Vaca originally sailed to Tampa Bay, Florida, as treasurer for the expedition of conquistador Pánfilo de Narváez (c. 1480–1528) in 1528. The expedition proved a disaster. Stranded without its ships, the landing party struggled to make boats for a voyage to New Spain, only to have the boats wrecked. Over two hundred men were lost; four survived. Led by Cabeza de Vaca, they walked across miles of desert in Texas and possibly as far west as California. Native Americans who valued them as healers helped keep them alive. They reached Mexico in 1536, full of strange tales of American Indian villages and unusual creatures called buffalo. He recorded his adventures in the first account of what is now the mainland United States, *Los naufragios* (*"The Shipwrecked Men"*, 1542).

Which Spanish explorer discovered the Mississippi River?

It was Hernando de Soto (c. 1500–1542). Lured by false reports of gold and silver treasures in the wilderness, he landed in Florida in 1539 and slogged through much of what is now the American South. He passed through present-day North and South Carolina, Alabama, Mississippi, and Tennessee. In 1541, he and his men became the first Europeans to see the mighty Mississippi River. The expedition also explored Arkansas, Oklahoma, and Texas, but de Soto did not live to complete it: he died of fever and was buried in the river he had discovered. Some of his men survived to reach Mexico in 1543.

Explorer Hernando de Soto is shown in his armor in this engraving. Despite the high temperatures in North America's south and southwest, Spanish explorers often wore their heavy armor into battle against Native Americans.

Did de Soto also discover the Grand Canyon?

No, that was another Spanish explorer, Francisco de Coronado (c. 1510–1554). He too came in search of rumored treasure—in this case, the fabulously wealthy Seven Cities of Cibola and another legendary realm named Quivira. Leading an expedition overland from Mexico in 1540, he explored what are now Arizona, New Mexico, Texas, Oklahoma, and Kansas. A party dispatched by Coronado and led by García López de Cárdenas was the first to view the natural splendor of the Grand Canyon.

However, natural splendor cannot fill pockets, and no great wealth was found. The magical cities turned out to be humble Native American villages. Spanish authorities were disappointed when Coronado returned empty-handed in 1542. More than fifty years passed before they tried to settle the territory he had explored.

Who were the Native Americans found by Coronado?

Some were the people whom the Spanish called **Pueblo** because of the **pueblos** (villages) in which they lived. Their flat-roofed, many-roomed houses were made of stone or adobe, a kind of clay brick. The Pueblos, who included groups like the Hopis and Tewas, were peaceful corn farmers skilled in weaving and pottery. Coronado visited their villages in Zuni, New Mexico, the basis for the legend of the Seven Cities of Cibola.

The legend of Quivira was based on the Wichita, a Kansas people encountered by Coronado, who lived in cone-shaped houses of grass. Other Native American groups of the American Southwest included the Apaches, who were warriors and hunters, and the Navajos, who combined hunting with agriculture. They and the many other American Indian groups of the region shared a belief in the sacredness of the land, a belief expressed in ritual and poetry.

The multistoried adobe dwellings of the Taos pueblo in New Mexico are believed to have been occupied by Native Americans for at least eight hundred years.

When did the American Indians of the Great Plains start riding horses?

The image of the American Indian hunting buffalo on horseback may seem eternal, but it isn't. There were no horses at all in the Americas until the Spanish conquistadors brought them. In 1540, Spanish explorer Francisco de Coronado, traveling through Kansas, let most of his 260 horses escape. The Great Plains Indians tamed the wild descendants of these horses and made them an important part of their culture.

If there was no great wealth in the American Southwest, why did the Spanish want to settle it?

In the game of colonization, the rule was "use it or lose it." Getting there first allowed you to claim possession, but if you didn't establish a colony, other countries could take it away from you.

In 1579, English navigator Francis Drake (c. 1540–1596) explored North America's Pacific Coast, reaching the vicinity of present-day San Francisco, California, and claiming the region for England. Spain realized that it had to occupy this

This woodcut shows Juan Ponce de León, who conquered Puerto Rico in 1508, governed it for four years, and came to Florida in 1513 seeking a fountain of youth. The 61-year-old explorer found death instead in a skirmish with Native Americans near present-day Tampa.

Western area, roughly consisting of present-day California, Arizona, New Mexico, Utah, and Nevada, as well as parts of Colorado, Wyoming, Kansas, and Oklahoma, or risk losing it to a rival.

The entire region of California, Arizona, New Mexico, and Texas was claimed by the Spanish and known as the "Far North." It also included present-day Nevada and Utah and parts of Colorado, Wyoming, Kansas, and Oklahoma.

The oldest public building still standing in the United States is the Governor's Palace in Santa Fe, New Mexico, the construction of which began in 1610.

When did Spain start founding colonies in what is now the American Southwest?

The first colony was founded in present-day New Mexico in 1598 by Juan de Oñate (c. 1550–c. 1630). He is considered the founder of New Mexico, called Nuevo Mexico by the Spanish and treated as a northern province of New Spain. Santa Fe, New Mexico's capital, was founded in 1609. A mission in Arizona, then considered part of New Mexico, was founded in 1692.

Signs of the Spanish

Nine U.S. states have Spanish names: Arizona, California, Colorado, Florida, Montana, Nevada, New Mexico, Oregon, and Texas. Spanish place-names can be found in North American localities from El Paso, Texas, to Campobello Island, New Brunswick, Canada. But perhaps the most intimate sign of the Spanish presence in early American history can be found in your wallet. The American dollar derives from the "Spanish dollar" or peso, a reliable unit of currency in colonial times. Even the dollar sign is believed to be of Spanish origin.

In the eighteenth century, French interest in Texas prompted Spain to found settlements there, including San Antonio in 1718. Rumors of Russian and British designs on California prompted Spain to found San Diego in 1769 and San Francisco in 1776.

Maine, Missouri, and New York each have a town called Mexico.

Where did Los Angeles get its name?

Now the largest city in California, Los Angeles was once a sleepy village on the Mexican frontier. It was founded in 1781 by provincial governor Filipe de Neve. Like many Latinos to the present day, he revered the Virgin Mary, so he named the place El Pueblo de Nuestra Señora la Reina de Los Angeles, Spanish for "the Village of Our Lady, the Queen of the Angels."

What is a presidio?

The word **presidio** is Spanish for "fort." Spanish settlements in the Far North usually centered on a mission church protected by soldiers in a presidio. The priests of the mission would try to convert the local Native Americans. One of the best-known mission priests was Junípero Serra (1713–1784), who founded many missions in California. Famous mission buildings include the Alamo in San Antonio, which later figured prominently in Mexican American history (see the chapter The Lost Land). The Spanish presidio in San Francisco later became a U.S. military base called the Presidio, and is now part of a national park.

Mexican Americans celebrate many religious holidays, some of them local events. The Festival of the Bells in San Diego, California, in July celebrates the founding of the Mission San Diego de Alcala in 1769.

New Mexicans who claim descent from the region's original Spanish settlers call themselves Hispanos to distinguish themselves from other Hispanic American goups. An example is Linda Chavez, who was executive director of the U.S. Commission on Civil Rights under President Ronald Reagan.

Who were the settlers who came to the Far North?

Although they came from New Spain, most were not of pure Spanish descent. Many were Native Americans of the Nahua group; others were mestizos. Most were poor people enticed to relocate in the Far North by offers of land. They eked out a difficult living farming and ranching, often in arid places that required irrigation. Local Native Americans such as the Pueblo were forced to work alongside them. Raids by other Native American groups such as the Apache were a constant threat. A revolt by the Pueblo in New Mexico almost expelled the Spanish permanently. Under such conditions, the colonies grew slowly. By 1800, for example, Texas had only about 3,500 settlers.

Who led the Pueblo revolt?

It was a medicine man named Popé, who refused to abandon his people's traditional religion and preached

This painting of Coronado and his troops was done by Frederic Remington, an American artist in the 1800s, who became famous for his pictures of the West.

Damn the Torpedoes!

Damn the torpedoes—full speed ahead!" is one of the best-known battle cries in American history. It was uttered by a Hispanic American of Minorcan descent: U.S. naval officer David Farragut (1801–1870).

His Spanish father, Jorge Farragut, immigrated from Minorca in 1772 and fought in the Revolutionary War. David exclaimed his famous line in 1864, during the Civil War battle of Mobile Bay. By "torpedoes" he meant not the modern underwater missiles but underwater mines planted in the path of his fleet. Farragut won the battle. For his heroism, he was made the first admiral of the United States.

The Farraguts belonged to a long line of Hispanic Americans who fought for their country. More than 300,000 Mexican Americans served in World War II. Seventeen won the Medal of Honor, five of them posthumously.

independence from Spain. Tired of exploitation by the Spanish, the Pueblo people did what he suggested. In 1680, the Pueblos revolted, killing more than four hundred New Mexico settlers and forcing the rest to retreat to El Paso, now part of Texas. Popé died in 1692, and in 1693 the Spanish recaptured Santa Fe. Centers of resistance remained, and the Great Pueblo Revolt was not entirely defeated until 1698.

What do the Canary Islands and Balearic Islands have to do with Spanish colonization of the Americas?

These two island groups, both owned by Spain, contributed colonists to the New World. In the eighteenth century, the Canary Islands, located off northwest Africa, sent colonists to San Antonio and San Saba, Texas; Louisiana; and Florida. When Florida was held by the British (1763–1783), the British recruited colonists for Florida from the Balearic Islands in the Mediterranean Sea.

One of the Balearic Island settlers was Esteban Benét from the island of Minorca. His descendant Stephen Vincent Benét (1893–1943) was a well-known twentieth-century poet and novelist.

Was Louisiana ever Spanish?

Although it was named for French king Louis XIV, this colony once belonged to Spain. The territory was first claimed for France in 1682. The French colony was vast, comprising the entire valley of the Mississippi River and its tributaries. It stretched from Montana to Ohio to Alabama to the present-day state of Louisiana. However, the French and Indian War (1754–1763) ended French possession of Louisiana. Britain won ownership of the section west of the Mississippi, while Spain got the regions to the east, as well as the port city of New Orleans. Spain kept possession until 1800, when the colony was ceded back to France.

Which came first: England's thirteen colonies on the Atlantic coast or Spain's colonies in the American Southwest?

The thirteen colonies that later became the United States began with the founding of Jamestown, Virginia, in 1607, England's first permanent settlement in North America. By that time, Juan de Oñate had already been living in New Mexico for nine years. However, Spanish colonization was slow. By the time San Francisco, California, was founded in 1776, England's thirteen colonies had not only been founded: they had grown, flourished, and were declaring their independence from their mother country.

An Amigo in New Orleans

Even before Spain entered the American War of Independence, one Spanish official was an **amigo**, or friend, to the rebels: Bernardo de Gálvez (1746–1786), who became governor of Louisiana in 1777. While Spain was still officially neutral, Gálvez saw to it that arms and supplies were sent to the rebels from New Orleans. After Spain declared war on Britain in 1779, Gálvez led and won several battles in the Southeast, including Baton Rouge and Natchez (1779), Mobile (1780), and Pensacola (1781). His efforts brought Florida back to Spain and kept the British redcoats busy, relieving pressure on George Washington's army. The city of Galveston, Texas, is named in his honor.

Did any Hispanics live in the thirteen English colonies?

Yes. Hispanics made up a small percentage of the colonial population. For example, New York contained a number of Jews descended from people who fled persecution in Spain and Portugal in the fifteenth century. New York's first Hispanic Jews had settled there in 1654, when it was still the Dutch colony of New Amsterdam.

Was Spain involved in the American Revolution?

American colonists were all alone when they began their rebellion against Great Britain in 1775. But they did not stay alone for long. France joined the war against Britain in 1778 and Spain in 1779. Soon the Netherlands and the ruler of Mysore in India were also firing on English troops.

France was the most generous ally. But Spain also helped, granting loans and financial guarantees to the rebels and opening Spanish ports as havens for American privateers. The Spanish navy fought at sea with the British, while Bernardo de Gálvez, the Spanish governor of Louisiana, waged war against the British in America (see sidebar).

The foreign allies of the United States grappled with Britain for their own reasons. Spain cared less about helping the American rebels than about winning back Florida. Spain had lost this colony to Britain in 1763 but got it back by war's end, along with West Florida: a strip of land on the coast of the Gulf of Mexico that included parts of what are now Alabama, Mississippi, and Louisiana. Regardless of Spain's motives, the fighting on many fronts tied down British forces, indirectly aiding the American cause.

If Spain got Florida back in 1783, why does Florida no longer belong to Spain?

Within a few years, Spain lost Florida, along with most of the rest of its American empire. The story of how that happened will be told in the next chapter.

ow much of the United States would be Spanish
pain had never lost any of its colonies? ◆ If Spain wa
o powerful, why did it lose all its American colonie
◆ What was the first colony Spain lost? ◆ When di
lorida become part of the United States? ◆ Wha
appened to the rest of Spanish America? ◆ How b
vas Mexico when it first became a nation? ◆ How di
he Lost Land get lost? ◆ Why did Americans want t
go to Texas, and why did Mexico want them there?
Why did Texas revolt against Mexico? ◆ What did th
phrase "Remember the Alamo" mean? ◆ When di
Texas become part of the United States? ◆ How di

THE LOST LAND

How much of the United States would be Spanish if Spain had never lost any of its colonies?

Had Spain kept its empire, North America would be a very different place. If you vacationed on the beaches of Florida, you would be on Spanish land. If you lived in San Francisco, California, or Santa Fe, New Mexico, you would be a resident of New Spain. Texas cowboys would be Spanish-speaking *vaqueros*, Lousiana crawfish would be a Spanish American dish, and the bison of the Great Plains would run on Spanish land. Dorothy, the Kansas girl in *The Wizard of Oz*, would have called New Spain home; so would Bill Clinton of Arkansas.

At the end of the eighteenth century, Spanish America was much larger and older than the United States. It included not only much of what is now the United States, but all of Mexico and Central America, along with most of South America and the West Indies.

If Spain was so powerful, why did it lose all its American colonies?

In the sixteenth century, Spain was the most powerful nation in the world. It had a strong monarchy and a fearsome military, funded by gold and silver from the American colonies. Then, like empires throughout history, Spain began to decline. England defeated the Spanish Armada, or naval fleet, in 1588. Endless wars and civil turmoil drained the country of money and manpower.

In 1588, Spain tried to conquer England with an armada, or fleet, of 130 warships. Aided by favorable weather and superior seamanship, the greatly outnumbered English navy defeated the Spanish Armada. About 60 Spanish ships were destroyed; no English ships were lost.

As vast as Spanish America was by the end of the eighteenth century, it was like a block of houses that is full of rebellious tenants and belongs to an absent landlord only on paper. Spain lacked the money, troops, or will to keep possession of what it claimed. In 1795, the losses began.

What was the first colony Spain lost?

The first colony to go was the first permanent colony Spain had founded: Santo Domingo, on the island of Hispaniola. In 1795, Spain ceded Santo Domingo to France. It would eventually become the Dominican Republic.

The second colony to be lost was Spain's most recent prize: Louisiana, acquired from France in 1763. In 1800, the French ruler Napoleon forced Spain to give it back. The United States bought it from France in 1803.

When did Florida become part of the United States?

Florida, with the Gulf Coast strip of land called West Florida, was the next chunk of Spanish America to be lost. In 1819, Spain ceded the Floridas to the United States, partly in return for American acknowledgment that Texas was part of New Spain. That acknowledgment was short-lived.

What happened to the rest of Spanish America?

Revolution soon drove Spain off the mainland of the Americas. By 1825, all of Spain's colonies in South America and Central America had rebelled and won their independence. Mexico became independent in 1821. All that was left of Spanish America were the West Indian colonies of Cuba and Puerto Rico. Both of these would be lost in the Spanish American War of 1898 (see the chapters Coming from Cuba and Coming from Puerto Rico).

How big was Mexico when it first became a nation?

With an area of 762,000 square miles, present-day Mexico is about one-fifth the size of the United States. But in 1821, the young country of Mexico included not only its present-day holdings but nearly one million square miles more, in the region called the Far North. This region

Happy Cinco de Mayo!

On Cinco de Mayo, or the Fifth of May, Mexican Americans celebrate their ethnic heritage with parades and parties. You might think it is the anniversary of Mexico's independence, but it isn't. That day is September 16, known as Diez y Seis, which commemorates the beginning of Mexico's war of independence from Spain in 1810. It was on this day that Miguel Hidalgo y Costilla (1753–1811), a priest in the village of Dolores, issued the Grito de Dolores ("Cry of Dolores"), a revolutionary call for land reform and racial equality. From that battle cry sprang a war that ended with Mexico winning independence in 1821.

Mexican Americans celebrate Diez y Seis, but Cinco de Mayo is an even more stirring occasion on which to remember their cultural background: something like St. Patrick's Day for the Irish. It commemorates the day in 1862 when Mexico defeated a French occupation force at the battle of Puebla. The French invaded Mexico in 1861 and were not fully driven out until 1867.

included the present-day American Southwest and part of the West, from California through New Mexico to Texas.

The Far North was sparsely populated. In 1848, when the bulk of it passed into American hands, there were only about 80,000 Hispanics living in it. To those Mexican Americans, stranded overnight in a foreign power's territory, it became known as the "Lost Land."

Present-day Mexico is divided into thirty-one states and the Federal District, which includes most of the capital, Mexico City.

How did the Lost Land get lost?

Mexico lost its northern provinces to the United States in a three-step process: the Texas Revolution, the Mexican War, and the Gadsden Purchase. The story begins with the first U.S. citizens in Texas. In 1822, Stephen F. Austin (1793–1836) led a group of American families to settle in the fertile region between the Brazos and Colorado Rivers in Texas. The move was authorized by the Mexican government.

Why did Americans want to go to Texas, and why did Mexico want them there?

American cotton farmers and cattle ranchers felt crowded as the population grew and cheap real estate became hard to find. They saw a promised land in the wide open spaces of Texas. As for Mexico, it did not so much desire Americans as it feared Europeans. Because Texas was thinly populated, Mexico worried that Britain or France would try to take it away—unless settlers could be found.

By 1830, more than 20,000 Americans were in Texas, outnumbering Mexicans by more than three to one. At this point, Mexico began to regret its liberal immigration policy. Texan Americans mostly governed themselves and ignored Mexican law. As the United States made offers to buy Texas, Mexico became worried about losing the state.

Why did Texas revolt against Mexico?

In 1835, Mexican president Antonio López de Santa Anna (1794–1876) threw out the nation's constitution and made himself dictator. Many Americans in Texas, as well as

Mexican soldiers under Santa Anna stormed into the Alamo on March 6, 1836, and killed all the rebels for Texan independence gathered inside. Their attack sparked even louder calls for Texan independence from Mexico.

In this engraving of the Battle of Buena Vista, fought February 23, 1847, General Zachary Taylor leads U.S. forces against the Mexican army, on the right. About 272 U.S. soldiers died and 387 were wounded in the encounter; 2,000 Mexicans died there.

Tejanos (Mexicans in Texas), hated this blow to their liberty. While most Tejanos wanted to remain part of Mexico, Texan Americans demanded full independence. In the Texas Revolution (1835–1836), independence was achieved.

What did the phrase "Remember the Alamo" mean?

The turning point of the Texas Revolution came in 1836 at a fortified mission called the Alamo. An army of several thousand Mexicans, led by dictator Santa Anna, laid siege to the fort and its 180 Texan rebels. The rebels included Juan Seguín and a company of Tejanos, along with such American frontiersmen as Davy Crockett, Jim Bowie, and William Travis. On March 6, after the rebels had refused Santa Anna's

A Blow for Slavery

The Texas Revolution is remembered as a blow for freedom. What is often forgotten is that many Texan Americans were southerners who owned slaves. In fact, Mexico's antislavery policy was one of the irritants that provoked the revolution. When Mexico abolished slavery in 1829, an outcry from Texans forced Mexico to take back the decree. In 1830, Mexico tried other measures to keep control of Texas, including limiting immigration, levying import taxes, and forbidding the slave trade. The new attempts to crack down on the "peculiar institution" of slavery only made Texans more rebellious.

order to surrender, the Mexican troops stormed the fort and killed all of the rebel soldiers.

Far from suppressing the rebellion, the massacre inflamed it. Texans rallied to the battle cry "Remember the Alamo!" Barely seven weeks later, at the Battle of San Jacinto on April 21, Texan forces defeated Santa Anna and forced him to recognize Texan independence.

When did Texas become part of the United States?

Many Americans in Texas were not satisfied with independence. They wanted to be reunited with their native country, the United States. Slave-owning American southerners wanted to annex Texas because it would enter the Union as a slave state, lending support to their side in the growing congressional disputes over slavery. In 1845, the United States annexed Texas as its largest state.

How did Mexico react to the annexation of Texas?

Mexico's congress never recognized Texan independence, arguing that General Santa Anna had granted it under duress. When the United States moved to annex Texas in 1845, Mexico cut off diplomatic relations, which is often a first step toward war.

Did war between Mexico and the United States follow annexation of Texas?

Not right away. Months went by, and the issue might have been settled peacefully, but U.S. president James K. Polk had reason to heat up the conflict—even at the cost of war. He wanted to acquire Mexico's entire Far North, the whole region from Texas to California. He and others like him believed that this expansion from coast to coast was America's "manifest destiny," an outcome plainly decreed by God. Among other things, expansion would give the United States rich trading ports on the Pacific Ocean and a land route to get to those ports.

In November 1845, Polk sent an emissary, John Slidell, to try to buy Mexico's northern regions. Still furious about Texas, Mexico refused. In 1846, one day after hearing about the refusal, Polk ordered General Zachary Taylor to move his forces from the Nueces River in Texas to the Rio Grande.

What did the Rio Grande have to do with starting a war?

Mexico claimed that the southern border of Texas was the Nueces River, but Texas claimed the true boundary was the Rio Grande, 150 miles further south. On hearing of Mexico's refusal to negotiate, President Polk stationed U.S. troops as deep as possible inside the disputed area—right on the banks of the Rio Grande.

If it was war he wanted, Polk did not have to wait long. General Taylor's army arrived at the Rio Grande on March 28, 1846. On April 25, a Mexican force attacked, killing or wounding sixteen American soldiers. On May 13, at Polk's request, the U.S. Congress declared war on Mexico. A subordinate of Taylor's named Colonel Hitchcock wrote: "It looks as if the government sent a small force on purpose to bring on a war, so as to have a pretext for taking California and as much of this country as it chooses."

Mexican general and dictator Santa Anna led an eventful career. He gained power as leader of the Mexican troops who defeated the Spanish at Tampico in 1829 and became president in 1833. His defeats in the Mexican War sent him into exile, but he returned to power in Mexico from 1853 to 1855, when he was forced into exile again. He remained in exile until his death in 1876.

The Bear Flag Republic

During the Mexican War, American explorer John C. Frémont (1813–1890) led a revolt against Mexico in Sonoma, California. With no support from the rest of the province, Frémont and other American settlers declared California an independent republic on July 4, 1846. The republic, which flew a bear flag, was short-lived. A few days later, the rebels turned their "country" over to the United States, and the bear flag was replaced with the American flag.

Henry David Thoreau wrote the 1849 essay "Civil Disobedience" to explain his refusal to pay taxes to support the Mexican War. Thoreau's doctrine of nonviolent resistance against injustice influenced twentieth-century political resisters Mohandas Gandhi and Martin Luther King Jr.

Was the Mexican War easy to win?

Not for the 13,000 Americans who died fighting it, most of them succumbing to disease in unhealthy camp conditions. Over a year's worth of battles were fought—most of them American victories, but some won at a high cost in casualties. Mexican troops were usually poorly disciplined and poorly led, but they outnumbered the Americans and fought ferociously. In 1847, many young cadets of the Chapultepec military school struggled to the death rather than surrender. They are still honored by Mexicans as *Los Niños Héroes*—"the boy heroes."

Zachary Taylor won battles at Palo Alto and Monterrey in northern Mexico. In New Mexico, U.S. forces captured Santa Fe. In California, the capture of Los Angeles was followed by a Mexican revolt that was suppressed. Final victory belonged to General Winfield Scott, who accepted the surrender of Mexico City in September 1847. It was the first time American troops had captured a foreign capital.

Did all Americans support the Mexican War?

The war was popular, especially in the South. As in the case of Texas, southerners hoped that slavery would expand into newly conquered territories, giving them more votes in Congress. But many Americans opposed the war, including then congressman Abraham Lincoln. Abolitionists, people who wanted to end slavery, were against the war because it threatened to create more slave states. And many considered it an unjust war of aggression against Mexico. These included writer and philosopher

Henry David Thoreau, who spent a night in jail in 1846 for refusing to pay taxes to support the war.

What was the result of the Mexican War?

In the Treaty of Guadalupe Hidalgo, signed on February 2, 1848, Mexico gave up its claim to Texas and accepted the Rio Grande boundary. It also ceded to the United States the vast region that included all of present-day California, Nevada, and Utah, along with most of Arizona and New Mexico. In return for this "Mexican Cession," the United States paid Mexico $15 million and assumed $3 million in unpaid claims of U.S. citizens against Mexico.

As a result of the Mexican War, the United States stretched to the shores of California. For the United States, this news was not all good. Controversy over whether the new territories should be slave or free was one of the main causes of the Civil War (1861–1865), the long, bloody conflict that divided North from South.

For Mexico, the news was all bad. Mexico lost about half of its territory, a region that had been home to Hispanic culture for over three centuries. The next chapter will show what the war meant for Mexicans already living on what was now U.S. soil, as well as for Mexicans who came later.

Why didn't the United States take all of Mexico?

Some Americans at the time thought it would be a good idea, but most were happy to only take half. The original goal had been to open a continental path from coast to coast, and that goal had been accomplished. Why drag out the war longer, trying to subjugate a rebellious population? It would seem too much like brute aggression. One American newspaper proudly declared, "[W]e take nothing by conquest....Thank God."

Who was Gadsden and what did he purchase?

You might think that the Mexican Cession would have been enough, but the United States wanted a little more. In 1853, the American minister to Mexico, James Gadsden (1788–1858), convinced Mexico to sell to the United States

"We never crossed a border. The border crossed us."

—Saying of *Tejanos* (Texans of Mexican origin)

the Mesilla Valley, including what is now Arizona and New Mexico. The price tag for the 30,000 square miles was $10 million. The aim of the purchase: mineral wealth and a route for a railroad that would bypass the Rocky Mountains. The Gadsden Purchase completed the story of American acquisition of Mexican land.

How many Mexicans lived in the territories that th
United States won in the Mexican War? ◆ Did th
Mexicans already living in the region go back to Mexico
◆ What was the Gold Rush and what did it mean fo
Mexican Americans? ◆ Who said, "Go west, youn
man"? ◆ What did Anglo Americans think of Mexica
Americans? ◆ Didn't the law protect Mexican America
property? ◆ What did Mexican Americans do on th
railroads? ◆ Is "buckaroo" a Spanish word? ◆ Di
Anglo miners learn anything from Mexican Americans
◆ Did bandidos really exist? ◆ What became of th
desperadoes? ◆ When were the first border patro

COMING FROM MEXICO

How many Mexicans lived in the territories that the United States won in the Mexican War?

In 1848, about 80,000 Mexicans lived in what was now the American West and Southwest. Of that number, about 60,000 lived in New Mexico, 13,000 in California, and 7,000 in Texas. Most were farmers and ranchers, with a sharp separation between the rich, educated property owners and the peons, or poor laborers, who worked for them.

Did the Mexicans already living in the region go back to Mexico?

A few did, but most did not. According to the Treaty of Guadalupe Hidalgo, which ended the Mexican War, Mexicans had one year to decide whether to move across the border to Mexico or stay in what was now a foreign land. Because they regarded the land as theirs, all but 2,000 decided to stay.

Those who stayed were guaranteed the rights of U.S. citizens, including the right to own property and to enjoy equal protection of the law. These rights would soon be violated.

What was the Gold Rush and what did it mean for Mexican Americans?

Just after the peace treaty was signed between the United States and Mexico in February 1848, startling news

During the Gold Rush, California's population swelled twentyfold in just four years: from 13,000 in 1848 to 260,000 in 1852.

Mexican American notables such as Pablo de la Guerra and Mariano Vallejo (1808–1890) helped to draft the constitution of the state of California, which entered the Union in 1850.

came from California. A mother lode, or large vein, of gold had been discovered at John Sutter's mill in the Sacramento Valley. By 1849, people from all over the world were coming to California to seek their fortune. The first of these "forty-niners" were Latinos from Peru and Chile, followed by Mexicans and Mexican Americans from throughout the Southwest. But Anglo Americans from the eastern United States soon outnumbered everyone else.

Who said, "Go west, young man"?

An Indiana journalist named John Soule (1815–1891) was the first to print the phrase, in 1851. But New York newspaper editor Horace Greeley (1811–1872) popularized the expression until people came to think he invented it. The West, said Greeley, was the place to "build up a home and fortune." After the Civil War ended in 1865, many Anglo Americans heeded his call: farmers, ranchers, miners, railroad magnates, businesspeople of every stripe. Prosperity followed for most of them, but not for most of the region's Mexican Americans.

What did Anglo Americans think of Mexican Americans?

Most Anglos were openly prejudiced against Mexican Americans, or Chicanos, regarding them as lazy, treacherous, and dishonest. Anglos despised them even more because they knew that many Mexican Americans were partly descended from American Indians. Since American Indians were regarded as subhuman, bigots thought that Mexican Americans must be less than human themselves.

Anglos were a little more respectful of rich Mexicans, particularly those who appeared to be of pure European descent. But even wealthy Mexican Americans had a hard time keeping their property as the tide of Anglos grew.

Didn't the law protect Mexican American property?

Although Mexican Americans were equal under the law to English-speaking Americans, they discovered that the law and reality were two different things. Laws were written only in English, with Spanish banned from the courtroom. Spanish and Mexican land grants were often not honored.

Sometimes the owner could not prove the exact boundaries of his land; sometimes he could offer no written proof of a grant made to his family centuries earlier. Even if a landowner won a lengthy court battle, he might have to sell his land to pay the lawyers.

Floods and droughts destroyed farms and killed cattle, adding to the woes of Mexican Americans. Anglos squatted (illegally occupied) on their land; violent men shot and lynched them. By the late nineteenth century, Chicanos were mostly a landless people. Many had no choice but to accept menial, low-paying jobs on farms, ranches, mines, and railroads.

What did Mexican Americans do on the railroads?

Large stretches of the railroads crisscrossing our nation were built or maintained by Mexican Americans. The Southern Pacific and Santa Fe lines hired Mexican Americans to build new desert lines in the 1880s. One reason the jobs were available was the Chinese Exclusion Act of 1882. This law, put in place by anti-Asian prejudice, halted Chinese immigration, which had previously supplied workers for the railroads. By 1929, it was estimated that 70 to 90 percent of workers on southwestern railroads were of Mexican origin.

Is "buckaroo" a Spanish word?

Sort of. This English word for cowboy is a corrupt form of the Spanish word "vaquero." The name fits, because Anglo cowboys learned a lot of their trade from Mexican Americans, who were experts in western-style ranching long before the Anglos arrived. Many of the cowboy techniques, equipment, and apparel we think of as distinctively American were actually copied from Latinos. The western saddle, chaps (or leather trousers), wide-brimmed hats to shield the face from the sun, the practices of rounding up and roping cattle on horseback—all these began with Mexican *vaqueros*.

Did Anglo miners learn anything from Mexican Americans?

In mining as in ranching, Mexican Americans knew more than the Anglo newcomers to the West and Southwest.

Many western words come from Spanish, including rodeo, lariat, lasso, mustang, *and* chaparral.

A group portrait of cowboys in the early twentieth century shows their ethnic and racial diversity. Many w
Mexican, and many were black. Mexican cowboys introduced many of the basics of western ranching.

The breed of dog called the Chihuahua was named for the Mexican state of Chihuahua, where the pint-sized animal was first identified around 1850. Some people think the Chihuahua descended from Native American breeds of dog, but it is more likely to have been imported from Asia by Spanish merchants.

Mexican Americans taught Anglos how to use a **batea**, a flat-bottomed pan, to extract gold from streams and rivers; how to pulverize gold-bearing rocks with a tool called an **arrastra**; and how to use mercury to refine gold.

Did bandidos really exist?

Yes, but the modern caricature of these nineteenth-century southwestern bandits as mere criminals is not quite accurate. To some, the **bandidos** were heroes. Also known as **desperadoes**, from the Spanish word *desesperado* ("desperate man") they began their outlaw careers in the 1850s. They included Juan Cortina in Texas and Joaquín Murieta, Juan Flores, and Tiburcio Vásquez in California.

Robbing, killing, rustling cattle, destroying property, the *bandidos* made Anglos and rich Mexican Americans quake in their boots. The rural poor, however, honored the bandits as rebels, providing them shelter from the law. Murieta was compared to Robin Hood, while people whispered of a

Desperado

Tiburcio Vásquez was born in 1835 in Monterey, California, Mexico. In 1848, when he was twelve, his part of Mexico became part of the United States. As he grew older, he realized that Anglo Americans did not respect him or his people. When he went to parties hosted by **Californios** (Californians of Mexican descent), Anglos would push their way through the gates, shoving him and his friends aside and forcing Chicana women to dance. He wrote that by the age of sixteen or seventeen, "a spirit of hatred and revenge took possession of me." Defending his people's honor in fights, he was always being chased by the police, until in 1852 he shot a constable. From then on he was an outlaw, a desperado.

He robbed stores and stage-coaches. He stole horses and cattle. Authorities launched a massive man-hunt, with the cooperation of rich *Californios*. But the Chicano peasants who sheltered him refused to betray him. He was their hero. Like Robin Hood, Vásquez was said to share his stolen goods with the poor.

In the 1870s, Vásquez was finally captured at the ranch of a man called Greek George. A jury of Anglos found him guilty, and he was hanged. Two weeks later, a supporter of Vásquez killed two Anglos who had helped capture the desperado. The war went on.

"Juan Flores Revolution." Vásquez was quoted as saying, "Given $60,000, I would be able to recruit enough arms and men to revolutionize Southern California."

What became of the desperadoes?

Aided by rich Mexican Americans, Anglo settlers organized posses and vigilante groups to hunt down the bandits. The effort was successful: by the 1870s, most of the bandits had been captured and executed. But the vigilantes were also indiscriminate, shooting and hanging people for no better reason than that they spoke Spanish. The Texas Rangers, organized during this period, became hated and feared by Mexican Americans for their violence against Hispanics.

When were the first border patrols established between Mexico and the United States?

Not until 1904 did the United States begin policing the border with Mexico. Even then, the aim of the patrol was not to keep out Mexicans but to keep out Asians who were trying to enter through Mexico. Because of anti-Asian sentiment, people from China and Japan were not allowed to make a home in the United States. Mexicans often came in search of temporary or permanent work, but were not counted as immigrants.

The idea that Mexicans could come "illegally" to a land that was once theirs is a relatively new one. Before it could become national policy, a few big changes had to happen.

When did Mexicans start coming to the United States in big numbers?

In the last decade of the nineteenth century, fewer than 1,000 Mexicans are estimated to have come to the United States. In the first decade of the twentieth century, the numbers jumped to about 50,000. From 1911 to 1920, the numbers increased to 219,000—and from 1921 to 1930, to 459,000. What happened?

After the Revolution

Porfirio Díaz ruled Mexico as a dictator for thirty-five years, from 1876 to 1911. Under his politically repressive reign, Mexico was modernized and business boomed. Foreign investors—including many from the United States—bought up Mexico's resources. But the vast majority of Mexicans remained poor, while the small circle of the rich got richer.

In 1910, Mexicans decided they had had enough. A violent revolution overthrew Díaz. For years, leaders such as Francisco Madero (1873–1913), Victoriano Huerta (1854–1916), and Pancho Villa (1878–1923) struggled among themselves for the soul of the revolution. Emiliano Zapata (1879–1919) led an army of Native Americans trying to repossess their land.

A new constitution, allowing for democratic elections, was enacted in 1917. Social reforms and land redistribution were mandated to benefit the poor. Some industries were nationalized and foreign holdings expropriated, or taken by the state.

Yet the gap between rich and poor never really went away. In recent years, the burden of foreign debt has made things worse, leading to high unemployment, inflation, and crime. Impoverished Mexicans continue to flock to the United States to try to escape their wretched condition.

Porfirio Díaz first came to prominence in the Mexican-American War of 1846–1848. He ran unsuccessfully for president in 1871 but was finally elected president in 1877 and again in 1884. He did not give up power until 1911, when he was forced to resign and flee to exile in Paris, France, where he died in 1915.

The most important change was the revolution that broke out in Mexico in 1910 (see sidebar). The revolution overthrew President Porfirio Díaz (1830–1915) and went on for years before its most violent phase ended in 1920. During that decade, chaos reigned in Mexico. Civil war raged, homes and property were destroyed, and over one million people were killed. Mexicans fled to the United States in droves.

Did all Mexican immigrants in the early twentieth century work as migrant farm laborers?

Then and now, many Mexican Americans have found work picking crops on big commercial farms. Field workers migrate from farm to farm, harvesting the crops that stock grocery stores and wind up on dinner tables. The labor is hard and low-paying, but for those with no property, education, or skills, it is better than starving.

It was not the only work Mexican Americans found in the early twentieth century. Some also worked on railroads, in copper and coal mines, and in factories. But the agricultural industry was their most important employer.

In 1994, a Native American group called the Zapatista National Liberation Army launched a short-lived revolt. Seeking social and political justice for the poor, they fought in the name of Emiliano Zapata, a hero of the Mexican Revolution.

Why was the agricultural industry important?

In the early twentieth century, commercial agriculture was booming in the West and Southwest. Small family farms were giving way to agribusiness—large, mechanized operations that could sell produce at low prices. New dams opened deserts to irrigation and planting. The invention of refrigerated train cars made it possible to ship fresh fruits and vegetables to America's growing cities. Investors saw lots of money to be made, and all they needed was cheap labor—workers who wouldn't demand to be paid very much.

In 1910, the first cotton was planted in California's Imperial Valley, which became a favorite place for Mexican immigrants to settle. In Texas and Arizona, cattle land was plowed up to make way for cotton planting. In Colorado, sugar beets became a big business. Other crops picked by Mexican Americans included grapes, melons, and citrus fruits.

What is a barrio?

Barrio is Spanish for "neighborhood." In the United States, it refers to a section of a city where Mexican

Child Labor

It is not unusual to see Mexican American children working alongside their parents in the California fields. Nearly one of every five crop pickers in the United States is under eighteen. The following passage comes from S. Beth Atkin's *Voices from the Fields: Children of Migrant Farm-workers Tell Their Stories*. It was written by nine-year-old José Luis Ríos, who lived with his parents, nine brothers and sisters, and other relatives in a small house in Las Lomas, California.

My parents work in la fresa [the strawberries] and la mora [the raspberries], and my mom sometimes packs mushrooms. During the week, they leave in the morning around six o'clock. I go and help them, mostly on weekends. I help pick the strawberries and put them in boxes. Last year my father took me to the fields a lot during the week, too, instead of bringing me to school....

The longest day in the field was when we picked a lot of strawberries. I felt bad and it was getting dark.... I said to my parents, "Let's go home," and finally they said, "We're going." It was hard to work so long. My body gets tired, and when it is muddy, my uncle has to park the truck far away, and I get tired and cold when I have to walk back to the truck.

Americans and other Latinos live. In the early part of this century, segregation often forced Mexican immigrants to settle in the barrios, even though these ghettos were dirty and dangerous. The one benefit was that Mexican Americans could stay close to other people who knew their native language and culture.

Is a colonia the same thing as a barrio?

Not quite. A **colonia** was literally a colony of Mexican Americans—a Hispanic community founded close to the farms, mines, or railroads where the immigrants worked. A *colonia* of boxcars and shacks would spring up every so often along the tracks that Mexican Americans were laying down. These settlements became the basis for some modern communities of Mexican Americans.

How did Mexican Americans already in the country react to the new wave of immigrants from Mexico?

Some welcomed the immigrants as brothers and sisters, but many were displaced. Descendants of the original settlers of California, New Mexico, or Texas were proud of their heritage, just like a northerner who can trace his lineage to the *Mayflower*. Some prosperous old-timers had only disdain for poor and uneducated newcomers. Others feared increased job competition.

Not all the newcomers were poor laborers. Some of the people fleeing the Mexican Revolution were members of the middle and upper classes. Because of money, education, and influence, they were generally able to establish a comfortable life in the United States.

What brought Pancho Villa to the United States?

The Mexican rebel leader came to the United States in 1916—but only for a short and bloody visit. In March 1916, angered at U.S. interference in the Mexican Revolution, Villa and his guerrillas crossed the border into New Mexico and killed sixteen people in the town of Columbus. President Woodrow Wilson responded by sending General John "Black Jack" Pershing and six thousand troops to capture Villa. Pershing crossed into Mexico and clashed with Mexican soldiers, but he never got his man.

Mutualistas, mutual aid societies, took shape in Mexican American communities early in the century. Members pooled their resources to offer loans, temporary housing, and employment assistance for Mexican immigrants in need of help. They also sponsored dances and other social events.

The parents of U.S. congressman Henry B. Gonzalez were middle-class people who fled the Mexican Revolution. A Democrat from Texas, Gonzalez formerly chaired the House Banking Committee.

Pancho Villa (center, on horse) may be remembered best as a guerrilla rebel, but before his bloody visit to the United States, he had been governor of the province of Chihuahua in 1913. U.S. troops who pursued him into Mexico had to withdraw because of Mexican president Carranza's opposition to their presence.

How did World War I affect Mexican Americans?

One effect of World War I, in which the United States took part from 1917 to 1918, was to encourage Mexican Americans to move north. With many men at war, northern factories experienced a shortage of labor. Moving north in search of industrial work, Mexican Americans were soon living in Chicago, New York, and elsewhere in the Midwest and Northeast.

When did Mexican immigration begin to be restricted?

Some restrictions began to appear early in the twentieth century. Mexican immigrants had to register and pay a tax at border stations; illiteracy, disease, or extreme poverty could disqualify them. Restrictions were tightened further in 1924. In that year, the United States launched a quota system for immigration from outside the Western Hemisphere, saying how many immigrants could come from each country. There was no quota for Mexico or any other country in the Americas, but immigration was made harder. Now would-be immigrants had to file applications, get passports and visas, and pay a number of fees. This was too expensive and difficult for the poor. Many began to immigrate illegally. Immigration controls became even tougher in 1929, when a combination of laws effectively banned immigration of laborers from Mexico.

How did illegal immigrants enter the United States?

The long border with Mexico was only lightly policed. With the help of **coyotes**, or professional smugglers of immigrants, many undocumented Mexicans made it across the border. Some hid in the backs of cars and trucks. Some waded across the Rio Grande, giving rise to the derogatory term "**wetback**."

American employers were often happy to give jobs to illegal immigrants. The bosses knew that illegal immigrants fearful of capture would work for even lower wages than legal ones. Employers sometimes hired coyotes to round up a fresh batch of illegal labor. Some farm owners would cheat undocumented Chicanos of their wages by exposing them to the police after they had harvested the crops but before they had been paid.

What happened to Mexican Americans during the Great Depression?

Mexican Americans suffered along with millions of other Americans during the economic catastrophe of the 1930s. Beginning in 1929 with the crash of the U.S. stock market, businesses closed, fortunes were wiped out, and many people, including Mexican Americans, were thrown out of work.

Mexican Americans also suffered something worse: the anger of Anglos who regarded them as foreigners taking away jobs and relief funds from "true" Americans. All across America, government and private agencies organized repatriation programs for sending Mexican Americans back to Mexico. About 500,000 Mexican Americans were encouraged, intimidated, or forced into leaving the country—the largest numbers from Texas, California, and the region of Indiana, Illinois, and Michigan. The Mexican government cooperated, setting up refugee camps to receive them.

Some of the repatriated people were undocumented workers, but many were legal residents or even U.S. citizens. Few Anglos protested, and few today even remember, the violations of civil rights associated with repatriation. But Mexican Americans stung by the injustice remembered.

Braceros got their name because they worked with their arms—bra-zos in Spanish. It was the equivalent of calling an employee a "hired hand."

Who were the braceros?

No sooner had repatriation removed Mexican Americans than the country wanted them back. When the United States plunged into World War II (1941–1945), the economic distress of the Great Depression ended. Citizens, unemployed and otherwise, were drafted into military service. Farms and factories came back to life to provide supplies for the troops. Suddenly there was a shortage of laborers to pick the crops. Who better to do the job than the same people who had done it before the Great Depression?

The United States and Mexico agreed in 1942 that Mexican laborers, called **braceros**, would be recruited to work here for a specified time. About 300,000 Mexican braceros took part in the program by the time the war ended.

Did the bracero program stop after the war?

No—it became bigger. American farm owners wanted to continue the arrangement, because the demand for farm produce was booming and braceros could be paid less than American workers. As a result, the program was kept alive from the end of the war until 1964. During that time, about 4.5 million braceros entered the country. Many became legal residents.

Did Mexican American immigration stop with the bracero program?

No. Heavy immigration from Mexico continued under the Immigration Act of 1965. By favoring applications from immigrants who already had family members living in the United States, the law encouraged Mexican Americans to bring family members from Mexico.

What is a zoot suit?

Take a very long coat with heavily padded shoulders, add baggy pants with a high waist and tight cuffs, and top it off with a broad-brimmed hat: that's a **zoot suit**. It helps if your hair is cut in a ducktail and you like to dance the jitterbug. The zoot suit was all the rage among urban youths in the 1940s, particularly African Americans and Chicanos.

What did zoot suits have to do with riots?

In June 1943, several young zoot-suiters believed to be Mexican American got involved in a brawl with U.S. Navy sailors on leave in Los Angeles. The rest of the ship's crew decided to take revenge. In the days that followed, sailors drove around the city in taxis, grabbing and beating every zoot-suiter they found. Young Mexican American men, whether wearing a zoot suit or not, were pulled out of buses and dragged from movie theaters to be beaten. Anglo civilians joined in the assaults. Police responded by arresting the victims.

The zoot suit riots spread to other cities, from California to Texas; from Chicago to Philadelphia to New York. When it was all over, a Los Angeles citizens' committee determined that racial prejudice was behind the riots. For the first time, Americans in high places began to see and investigate the racism of Anglos against Mexican Americans. Chicanos began to realize that their very right to exist was in danger. They had to unite and become politically active as advocates in their own behalf.

When did Mexican Americans start organizing politically?

The first major organization was the League of United Latin American Citizens (LULAC), founded in Texas in 1929. This Mexican American organization sought to protect the civil rights of Mexican Americans and ensure equal opportunity for education and employment. The Community Service Organization (CSO), founded in the late 1940s, emphasized citizenship and voter registration drives to elect Mexican Americans to office. It succeeded in electing Edward R. Roybal to the Los Angeles city council in 1949. Similar organizations, such as the Mexican American Political Organization (MAPA), followed in the 1950s. In Crystal City, Texas, in 1963, the Political Association of Spanish Speaking Organizations (PASSO or PASO) managed

"Dogs and Mexicans Not Allowed!"

—Sign posted in the American south in the 1960s, according to visiting Colombian writer Gabriel García Márquez

to elect a town council that was exclusively Mexican American.

Who was César Chávez?

Born in Yuma, Arizona, César Estrada Chávez (1927-1993) was a migrant farm worker and the son of migrant farm workers. Moving often with his family, he attended sixty-five elementary schools and never graduated from high school. He knew firsthand the dismal poverty and injustice suffered by Chicano farm workers. He decided to do something about it by becoming a labor organizer.

Chávez founded a union called the United Farm Workers (UFW). From 1965 to 1970, the UFW carried out a strike demanding higher wages from growers of table grapes in California. *La Huelga*, or "the Strike," drew national attention to the plight of Chicano farm workers: the shacks where they were forced to live; the pesticides that endangered their lives; the violence used to intimidate them.

A follower of Indian resistance leader Mohandas Gandhi, Chávez insisted on nonviolence from his union

César Chávez (center) worked all his life for migrant farm-worker unions. After he successfully led a strike on behalf of grape harvesters, he continued his efforts for other workers, including lettuce pickers.

members, even when beaten or jailed. Calling for a national boycott to support *La Causa*, or "the Cause," he persuaded millions of Americans not to buy California table grapes. In the end, the growers gave in to union demands. Mexican Americans had achieved a new level of self-respect and community awareness.

Besides César Chávez, have any other children of migrant farm workers become famous?

One who did is stage and film writer and director Luis Valdez. He was born into a Chicano family of migrant farm workers in 1940. In 1965, to support the United Farm Workers strike led by César Chávez, Valdez founded a theater company known as Teatro Campesino, which dramatized the plight of farmworkers in plays and films. He became nationally known for writing and directing the 1978 play *Zoot Suit*. The play dramatized a real-life 1940s criminal case known as the Sleepy Lagoon incident, in which several Mexican Americans were wrongfully convicted of murder as a result of racial basis. In 1987, Valdez directed the movie *La Bamba*.

La Bamba

In 1959, the traditional Mexican song "La Bamba" was transformed into a foot-stomping rock'n'roll hit by Chicano singer Ritchie Valens, born Richard Valenzuela in Los Angeles in 1941. The song's Latin chord sequence became a standard piece of rock vocabulary in such later songs as "Twist and Shout" (1960). Valens's career was cut tragically short when he died in a plane crash in 1959.

Valens gained a whole new audience in 1987, when a movie about his life, entitled *La Bamba*, was released. Among the makers of the film were several Mexican Americans. The director was Chicano activist Luis Valdez. The title song was recorded by the Mexican American group Los Lobos. The film's musical director was Carlos Santana, who was born in Mexico—although he is mainly known for the Afro-Cuban rhythms in such songs as "Evil Ways."

However, the main character of *La Bamba* was portrayed not by a Chicano but a Filipino American: Philippine-born actor Lou Diamond Phillips, whose mixed heritage includes Hispanic descent.

Captain Kirk's archnemesis Khan in Star Trek II: The Wrath of Khan *(1982) was played by Mexican-born Ricardo Montalban, who also starred on the TV show "Fantasy Island." His brother Carlos Montalban was the TV pitchman El Exigente for Savarin coffee.*

Is Edward James Olmos the son of migrant farm workers?

No. Born in Los Angeles in 1947, the film star is the son of a Mexican-born welder. He grew up in a tough barrio and never forgot the problems of urban Chicanos. He was a Tony nominee for his performance in the play *Zoot Suit* and became well-known in the 1980s for the TV series "Miami Vice." He portrayed real-life Chicano math teacher Jaime Escalante in the film *Stand and Deliver* (1988). Committed to fighting drugs and gang violence, he dramatized his social concerns in *American Me* (1992), which he directed and starred in.

What was the first important Chicano novel?

It was *Pocho* by José Antonio Villarreal, published in 1959. Based partly on the author's life, the novel tells the story of a Chicano youth growing up in California's Santa Clara valley. Other respected books by Mexican American authors include *Bless Me, Ultima* (1972) by Rudolfo Anaya; *Woman Hollering Creek and Other Stories* (1991) by Sandra Cisneros; *And the Earth Did Not Part* (1971) by Tomás Rivera; *Hunger of Memory* (1982) by Richard Rodríguez; and *Bloodroot* (1982) by Alma Villanueva.

Why do so many Chicano artists paint murals?

Painting on walls has a rich history in Mexico, whose world-famous mural painters include Diego Rivera (1886–1957) and José Clemente Orozco (1883–1949). Mural painting is seen as a form of public education and inspiration. Mexican American artists have carried on the

Who Are You Calling "Pocho"?

The word in the title of José Villarreal's novel *Pocho* is a derogatory term used by people in Mexico to describe Mexican Americans. It suggests a Mexican who has foolishly given up his ethnic heritage to seek his fortune among the Anglos, who look down on him. The term implies "stupid" or "small." Chicanos often face prejudice not only from Anglos but from Mexicans who regard them with this kind of contempt.

tradition, often depicting images such as Our Lady of Guadalupe, Aztec symbols, and historical scenes like the Spanish conquest and Mexican Revolution. Chicano muralists include Judy Baca, Manuel Martínez, and Margo Oroña. Graffiti painted by young Chicanos on walls and underpasses is sometimes seen as a popular variety of mural painting.

Who were the Brown Berets?

Founded in East Los Angeles in 1967, they were one of many Chicano groups in the 1960s who went even further than Chávez in demanding change. Such groups embraced the name "Chicano"—originally a derogatory term for Mexican Americans—as a badge of honor. They spoke of themselves as brown rather than black or white. The Brown Berets were a paramilitary organization of youths who wore brown berets and took part in public protests. They emphasized the separateness of Mexican Americans and the need to protest Anglo oppression—even to the point of revolution.

They were not the only Chicano youths protesting. All over the Southwest, Chicano students demanded better educational facilities and more courses on Mexican American culture and history. In 1968, many organized high school walkouts to press their demands.

Did Chicano activists ever use armed force?

Some did. Reies López Tijerina, who founded the Alianza Federal de Mercedes (Federal Alliance of Grants) in 1963, believed that Chicanos should take back the "lost land" that had belonged to them before the Mexican War. When legal appeals failed, his group of 20,000 Alianza members—*aliancistas*—turned to direct action.

In 1966, the Alianza tried to take over part of Kit Carson National Forest in New Mexico. In the following years, they tried to make citizen's arrests of prominent officials, including New Mexico's governor. *Aliancistas* engaged in shoot-outs with police and were hunted with tanks and helicopters. In 1970, Tijerina was sent to prison for two years. His Alianza did not succeed in its efforts, but it helped draw national attention to Chicano issues.

Where is Aztlán?

In the Aztec religion, it is the mythical homeland of the Aztecs. To Chicano activists in the 1960s, it was a name for the American Southwest. In 1969, Chicano boxer, poet, and movement leader Rodolfo "Corky" González made it the focus of *El Plan Espiritual de Aztlán*, the "Spiritual Plan of Aztlán." This plan, supported by many Chicano organizations, called for creation of a separate Mexican American state in the Southwest. González founded the Crusade for Justice in Denver and wrote the influential poem "I am Joaquín."

Who founded La Raza Unida?

The Mexican American political party La Raza Unida was founded in 1970 by José Angel Gutiérrez. Less radical than González, Gutiérrez wanted to work within the American political system to elect Chicano candidates to public office. To some extent, the efforts of La Raza Unida and similar organizations have succeeded. By now, hundreds of Mexican Americans have been elected or appointed to national, local, and state offices.

Are many Mexican Americans still poor?

As of 1998, the World Almanac reported that 28 percent of Mexican Americans—more than one out of four—lived

Behind the Miranda Warnings

At some point in almost every police movie and TV show, the police read a suspect the "Miranda warnings." Suspects are warned they have the right to remain silent, that anything they say can be used against them, that they have the right to an attorney, and that an attorney will be appointed if they cannot afford one.

The ritual reading of these rights stems from a 1963 case in which Ernesto Miranda, an Arizona Hispanic, was convicted of rape based on his confession to the police. The U.S. Supreme Court threw out the conviction, saying that Miranda's confession could not be used against him because he had not been informed of his rights. Since then, police have been careful to inform suspects of their Miranda rights.

As for Miranda, he was retried and convicted again based on different evidence. Paroled in 1972, he was killed four years later in a bar fight.

below the poverty level. Many of these are recent immigrants, and it is possible that education will help raise them from poverty. But the high school dropout rate among Mexican Americans is 50 percent—a problem rooted in poverty that makes continued poverty more likely.

How many Mexicans have immigrated to the United States during the twentieth century?

From 1900 to 1990 about 3.5 million Mexicans immigrated legally to the United States. Many more are believed to have come illegally. Because unemployment and destitution are perennial problems in Mexico, it is expected that Mexicans will continue to immigrate in large numbers. Some Mexicans migrate back and forth between the two countries, going wherever jobs or family ties might lead them.

How many people are caught each year trying to cross into the United States from Mexico without documents proving their legal status?

The Border Patrol catches about one million each year, sending most of them back to Mexico. Most are Mexicans, though some come from other parts of Latin America, particularly Central America. Those who are caught and sent back to Mexico often return to try another day. Although the Border Patrol monitors the border with everything from helicopters to movement sensors to night-vision goggles, many still slip past.

Is there a wall or fence that separates Mexico from the United States?

In some places there is. At Tijuana, Mexico, a ten-foot-high steel wall separates the two countries—a wall that people climb over every day. There has been talk of building a barrier across the entire two-thousand-mile border, something like the Great Wall of China. But the project would be expensive and, to some, a sad comment on relations between the two countries.

Where do most Mexican Americans live?

There are Chicano communities all over the country, but the majority of the nation's 13.5 million Mexican

A posada is a Mexican American Christmas pageant reenacting the efforts of the expectant Virgin Mary and her husband Joseph to find an inn that would take them on Christmas Eve. In Spanish, the word means "hotel" or "inn."

Americans still live in California, Texas, New Mexico, and Arizona—the states that border, and once belonged to, Mexico. Their culture forms an important part of that area's character.

What do you get if you break a piñata?

You get candy and toys. A **piñata** is a decorated container of clay or papier-mâché full of such objects. As it hangs from the ceiling, blindfolded children try to break it with long sticks. If they break it, the candies and toys spill out, and everybody grabs what they can. This traditional Mexican game is a favorite at Mexican American birthday parties and other **fiestas**, or celebrations.

Can curanderas cure the sick?

Many Mexican Americans believe they can. **Curanderas** are folk healers, usually women, who combine Catholic faith-healing with herbology and ancient Aztec and Mayan beliefs. Many people swear by their powers to cure illness, and some southwestern clinics keep them on staff. Some are also **parteras**, or midwives, who assist at births.

What is a mariachi band?

It is a Mexican or Mexican American band that walks around playing traditional Mexican songs on guitars, violins, and sometimes trumpets. The musicians wear brightly sequined Spanish costumes and large-brimmed sombreros, or hats. Evolving from rural Mexican origins, **mariachi**

The Day of the Dead

Don't be surprised to see skeletons on the homes of Mexican Americans on the days after Halloween. Mexican Americans celebrate November 2 as *El Día de los Muertos* ("the day of the dead"). This is the same day as the Roman Catholic feast of All Souls' Day, when the church prays for departed souls in purgatory. Mexican Americans take the day seriously—not just praying but going out to cemeteries with gifts of food and flowers for the dead. Still, a spirit of festiveness prevails, as people put up skeletons symbolizing the dead.

bands became internationally popular in the mid-twentieth century as a musical emblem of Mexico.

Some Mexicans celebrate the Day of the Dead by constructing elaborate scenes. This group is particularly high-spirited.

Why did Linda Ronstadt record a Spanish-language album?

Because she is part Hispanic. Born in Tucson, Arizona, in 1946, she is a blend of German and Mexican. From the time of her first number-one hit, "You're No Good," in 1974, her Anglo-sounding name concealed her ancestry from many of her fans. Her 1987 album *Canciónes de mi padre* (Songs for My Father), in which she recorded Mexican folk songs in Spanish, made her heritage clear.

Who are some other Mexican American singers?

Two of the most famous ones use Anglo-sounding stage names. Freddy Fender was born Báldemar Huerta; Vikki Carr was born Florencia Cardona. Both openly embrace their Mexican American heritage. In songs such as

Mexican jumping beans really do jump. These beans are actually shrub seeds that are infested with moth larvae. The movement of the larva inside causes the bean to roll and jump.

Mexican American Foods

A tortilla ("little cake") is a flat, round bread, like a pancake, made from cornmeal or wheat flour and baked on a hot surface.

A burrito (meaning "little donkey" in Spanish) is a soft flour tortilla wrapped around meat, beans, or cheese.

An enchilada ("in chili") is a soft flour tortilla wrapped around meat and cheese and served with a topping of tomato-chili sauce.

A fajita ("little band" or "strip") is marinated, grilled meat served in a tortilla.

A taco ("plug" or "wad") is a hard corn tortilla folded around ground meat, beans, or cheese.

A tamale (the Native American name of the dish) consists of fried, chopped meat and crushed peppers that have been rolled in cornmeal dough, wrapped in corn husks, and steamed.

"Before the Next Teardrop Falls" (1975), Fender displayed the unique brew of country, blues, and Mexican folk known as **Tex-Mex** music. Carr won a Grammy in 1991 for her album *Cosas del Amor.*

What was Selena's full name?

The Mexican American singer was born Selena Quintanilla Perez. She became a huge star of **Tejano** music, a subculture that was then little known outside of Texas and the Hispanic American community. On March 31, 1995, a disgruntled employee shot her to death. The public mourning of her many fans and the subsequent movie biography *Selena* made her much better known to Americans at large.

Are sweet red peppers and red hot chili peppers related?

Yes. The big, sweet fruits found on pizzas and salads and the long, skinny, mouth-burning peppers found in Mexican restaurants both belong to the genus Capsicum. Both are native to Latin America. Chili peppers are especially popular in Mexico, which is home to about two hundred varieties. Ground into powder or stirred into chili sauce, the peppers are part of many Mexican American dishes, including **chili con carne**.

The English word "barbecue" comes from the Spanish word barbacoa, which in turn comes from an Arawak word. A traditional Mexican barbacoa involves cooking a whole lamb or goat for hours in a pit lined with heated stones.

Did chili con carne originate in Mexico?

No. It first appeared in the United States, among Mexican Americans in San Antonio, Texas, about 1880. The name means "chili peppers with meat," though the hearty mix of beans, chili peppers, and spices is also available nowadays in vegetarian form. Chili was first sold in canned form in Texas about 1908. Oddly, the person who canned and sold it was a German American.

What's the difference between a taco and an enchilada?

These and other Mexican dishes are found today in restaurants and supermarket freezers across the United States, but Americans still have trouble telling them apart. Most of them originated with the Native Americans who lived in what are now northern Mexico and the American Southwest. People in Mexico regard them as appetizers, side dishes, or fast foods rather than main courses.

A taco is a hard corn tortilla folded around meat, beans, or cheese. An enchilada is a soft flour tortilla wrapped around meat or cheese, and topped with a tomato-chili sauce.

What do Mexicans consider their national dish?

Tacos and enchiladas are better known, but the dish that stands in highest regard among Mexicans and Mexican Americans is turkey in a **mole poblano** sauce. This thick sauce combines many flavors, including chili peppers, garlic, bananas, onions, and unsweetened chocolate. The dish should be served with tortillas or enchiladas.

How far is Puerto Rico from the mainland United States? ◆ Is Puerto Rico just one island? ◆ Why did Spain want to keep Puerto Rico? ◆ Why did Puerto Ricans revolt against the Spanish? ◆ Why do Puerto Ricans celebrate El Grito de Lares? ◆ Why did the United States invade Puerto Rico? ◆ How did Puerto Ricans feel about the American invaders? ◆ When did the people of Puerto Rico become U.S. citizens? ◆ Who was the first Puerto Rican elected governor of Puerto Rico? ◆ Did Puerto Rico become richer or poorer under the United States? ◆ What was Operation Bootstrap? ◆ Are Puerto Ricans on the island still poor? ◆ Wh

COMING FROM PUERTO RICO

How far is Puerto Rico from the mainland United States?

This mountainous, tropical island in the Caribbean Sea is about one thousand miles southeast of Miami, Florida. At one hundred miles long and thirty-five miles wide, it is not quite as big as Connecticut. It is a little more populous than Connecticut, with about 3.8 million people.

Is Puerto Rico just one island?

The Commonwealth of Puerto Rico, a self-governing possession of the United States, actually consists of four islands. These are the main island of Puerto Rico and three islets: Mona, Vieques, and Culebra. For nearly four centuries before becoming a U.S. possession, Puerto Rico belonged to Spain. Spain held on to Puerto Rico and Cuba long after its other American colonies revolted and won their independence.

Why did Spain want to keep Puerto Rico?

In colonial times—from the early sixteenth to early nineteenth centuries—Puerto Rico was important for military reasons. Puerto Rico is the easternmost of all the large West Indian islands known as the Greater Antilles. Ships traveling to and from Spain's colonial ports in the Caribbean and Gulf of Mexico had to pass Puerto Rico.

The only tropical rain forest under the care of the United States Forest Service is in Puerto Rico. Called El Yunque, it receives about 240 inches of rain a year and contains 250 kinds of trees. About 30 of these grow nowhere else in the world.

In Spanish colonial times, San Juan, the capital of Puerto Rico, was guarded by no fewer than three forts, including El Morro, now a popular tourist attraction.

Recognizing its strategic value, several nations tried to capture it in colonial times, including England. But Puerto Rico stayed Spanish. Puerto Rico gradually became a rich agricultural colony, exporting sugar, coffee, tobacco, ginger, and cattle. Its native Arawak population died out quickly because of Spanish cruelty and exploitation. But new workers replaced them: slaves from Africa, brought to the island as early as the 1510s. The Africans worked the plantations of the rich and contributed to the mixed racial stock of Puerto Rico.

Why didn't Puerto Ricans revolt against the Spanish?

Puerto Rico was a small island colony heavily dependent on its mother country. Perhaps for that reason, it stayed loyal to Spain when other larger, more self-sufficient colonies were fighting wars of independence. In fact, in the early nineteenth century, the island was a haven for loyalists fleeing revolutions in other Spanish American colonies.

By the 1820s, Puerto Rico and Cuba were the last remnants of Spain's once great American empire. Puerto Rican patriots such as Ramón Power and José Maria Quiñones wanted greater autonomy, or self-rule. But they were willing to work within the framework of the Spanish constitution, which had recently been made more liberal. The king's power was curtailed by the *Cortes*, or parliament. Spain, however, was slow in treating Puerto Ricans as citizens entitled to political representation. For decades, Puerto Rico was ruled by military governors.

Many Names for One Island

San Juan, Puerto Rico's capital city, is named for San Juan Bautista, or Saint John the Baptist. This was the name Christopher Columbus gave the island when he first landed there in 1493. Conquistador Juan Ponce de León gave it its present-day name of Puerto Rico, or "Rich Port."

There is yet another name for Puerto Rico: *Borinquen*. Meaning "land of the brave lord," this was what the original Arawak natives called their island. To this day, *Borinquen* is an informal name for Puerto Rico, and *Boricua* is another name for a Puerto Rican.

These Cuban soldiers were among those who fought against the United States in the Spanish American War. When Spain lost the war, its colonies, including Puerto Rico, fell under U.S. control.

Why do Puerto Ricans celebrate El Grito de Lares?

This holiday commemorates the night of September 23, 1868, when Puerto Ricans took over the town of Lares and demanded independence from Spain. The revolt was crushed, but the "cry of Lares" had been heard. Slavery was abolished in 1873, and in 1897 the Spanish crown agreed to give Puerto Rico limited autonomy. The island would have its own law-making parliament, though Spain reserved the right to disband it at will. Would the new government have worked? No one knows. On July 25, 1898, before the government could take power, the United States invaded Puerto Rico.

Why did the United States invade Puerto Rico?

From April to August 1898, the United States waged a war with Spain called the Spanish American War. The United States went to war in part to help Cuba win its struggle for independence from Spain (see the chapter Coming from Cuba). But the war was also prompted by American imperialists who wanted the United States to become a world power, with overseas colonies and global interests. The empire builders got their way. As a result of the Spanish American War, the United States won control of Cuba, Puerto Rico, and Spain's South Pacific colonies of

Guam and the Philippines. Cuba and the Philippines have since become independent countries, but Guam and Puerto Rico are still U.S. possessions.

How did Puerto Ricans feel about the American invaders?

Spanish forces on the island were defeated in about three weeks. Puerto Ricans offered little resistance. They were glad to see Spanish rule end, and were hopeful that the United States would support their wish for self-government. To their disappointment, they were not even consulted when Spain ceded Puerto Rico to the United States. Under the Foraker Act of 1900, the island was administered as a U.S. territory, overseen by a governor who was appointed by the president. Puerto Ricans were not American citizens and had less autonomy than before. They became subject not to Spanish-speaking people but to rulers who spoke a foreign language and had a different culture. They continued to demand a greater say in their own government.

When did the people of Puerto Rico become U.S. citizens?

On March 2, 1917, when President Woodrow Wilson signed the Jones Act, all Puerto Ricans became U.S. citizens, except the few who refused to accept citizenship. Wilson was motivated in part by the need for more soldiers to fight World War I. As citizens, Puerto Ricans were now eligible for the draft. Thousands were soon serving in the armed forces.

Although they were U.S. citizens, Puerto Ricans did not have to pay federal income tax and did not vote in national elections. Their House of Delegates was still controlled by the appointed American governor.

In the late 1930s, a brief uprising against U.S. rule broke out in the city of Ponce. Nineteen people died. It reminded American authorities that Puerto Rico's situation had to change.

Theodore Roosevelt Jr. (1887–1944)— son of the U.S. president of the same name—was governor of Puerto Rico from 1929 to 1932.

Who was the first Puerto Rican elected to govern Puerto Rico?

In 1946, the United States appointed a native Puerto Rican, Jesús T. Piñero, as governor. But the first Puerto Rican to be elected to the post was Luis Muñoz Marín (1898–1980). A journalist educated in Washington, D.C., he was the son of Luis Muñoz Rivera (1859–1916), a patriot who had agitated against Spanish rule. In the late 1930s, the younger Muñoz founded the Popular Democratic Party and agitated against U.S. rule. In the 1940s, he changed his views, working instead for the transformation of the island into a self-governing commonwealth. He believed that the economic advantages of the link to the wealthy United States out-weighed whatever gains might result from independence—as long as Puerto Ricans could govern themselves.

The transformation to commonwealth was completed on July 25, 1952. In that year, under a new constitution, Puerto Rico's own elected governor and legislature were fully put in charge of the island's internal affairs. The United States would continue managing its foreign affairs. Muñoz was elected—and three times reelected—governor (1949–1965). He was the first native-born Puerto Rican governor to be put in office by the people's vote. July 25, Constitution Day, remains a Puerto Rican holiday.

Did Puerto Rico become richer or poorer under the United States?

At first it became poorer. In the first few decades after the Spanish American War, American businesses flocked to Puerto Rico to convert much of the agricultural land to sugar production. Farmers who had been growing their own food now worked at growing sugar. Their employment—and their ability to feed their families—depended on the price of sugar, which was subject to drastic change. Unemployment boomed in Puerto Rico, particularly in the Great Depression of the 1930s.

The problem of poverty was made worse by a population boom. The United States introduced health and sanitation measures that saved children and adults from dying. But the same measures allowed the population to double from about one million to two million in the early twentieth century.

What was Operation Bootstrap?

Led by Governor Muñoz in the 1950s, it was an eco-nomic program aimed at relieving Puerto Rico's poverty.

Recalling the old expression "lifting oneself up by the boot-straps," the program sought to build a modern industrial base for a country that had long been agricultural. The program encouraged U.S. manufacturing firms to set up operations in Puerto Rico. Businesses that did so were rewarded with exemption from various federal taxes.

As a result of Bootstrap and other programs, Puerto Rico has become highly industrialized. Most of its people are now city dwellers working in manufacturing and service industries. Pharmaceutical companies and the tourism business are among the largest employers. Only 3 percent of Puerto Ricans on the island still work in agriculture.

Are Puerto Ricans on the island still poor?

They are by comparison to other Americans. Puerto Rico's 1995 per capita gross product of $7,662 was about a third of the average U.S. citizen's income on the mainland. However, Puerto Rico is well-off by Latin American standards. For example, Puerto Rico's per capita gross product is nearly twice as high as the Dominican Republic's and six times as high as Cuba's.

What president was nearly assassinated by Puerto Rican terrorists?

President Harry S Truman was nearly shot on November 1, 1950, by two Puerto Rican nationalists desperate to win independence for their homeland. He escaped unharmed. Just four years later, on March 1, 1954, three Puerto Rican **independentistas**, or independence activists, attacked the U.S. Capitol. Two were men—Rafael Candel Miranda and Andrés Cordero; one was a woman, Lolita Lebrón. The three terrorists fired guns from the gallery of the U.S. House of Representatives, wounding five congressmen. The attempted assassins were put in prison until 1979. Miranda, their leader, became a lifelong hero of the independence cause.

Are there still people in Puerto Rico who want independence?

Yes, but they are few in number. When Puerto Rican voters were asked in 1993 to choose among independence, statehood, or continued commonwealth status, only 4 per-cent chose independence. However, the *independentistas* have often been highly visible. In 1983, a terrorist national-ist group called Los Macheteros made headlines when it robbed $1.7 million from an armored car company in West Hartford, Connecticut.

The name of the terrorist group Los Macheteros means "bearers of machetes," traditional swords used by Carib-bean farmers to cut sugarcane.

Why isn't Puerto Rico a state?

The main reason is that Puerto Ricans have voted against becoming one. Statehood has certain disadvantages for Puerto Ricans. Because tax exemption for U.S. businesses would end, companies would probably leave the island, throwing people out of work. On the other hand, statehood would give Puerto Rico full representation in Congress.

The question was put to Puerto Ricans in a plebiscite, or direct popular vote, in 1964 and 1993. Both times Puerto Ricans voted in favor of remaining a commonwealth. However, in the 1993 vote, the movement for statehood gained ground: 46.3 percent of voters wanted statehood, only a little less than the 48.6 percent who wanted com-monwealth status. With a margin that narrow, the vote might easily go the other way in the next vote, scheduled for late 1998.

If the movement for statehood prevails, Puerto Rico might become the nation's fifty-first state. If so, it would be the first state with an almost entirely Hispanic population. The idea is not unthinkable. Millions of Puerto Ricans who have left the island already live within the fifty states.

When did Puerto Ricans start migrating to the U.S. mainland in large numbers?

Puerto Ricans have been coming to the mainland throughout the twentieth century. But the "Great Migration" of Puerto Ricans to the mainland began in the mid-1940s, at the end of World War II, and lasted until the middle of the 1960s. Crowded conditions and unemployment on the island stirred many Puerto Ricans to move to the United States, which was enjoying an economic boom in those years. Inexpensive airline travel made it easy: Puerto Ricans were the first large group of newcomers to come to the United States by airplane.

From 1940 to 1950 alone, the number of Puerto Ricans in the United States more than tripled, from 70,000 to 226,000. Since the 1960s, migration from Puerto Rico has continued, though at a slower pace. More than two million people of Puerto Rican ancestry now live on the U.S. mainland. This is more than half as many Puerto Ricans as live on Puerto Rico.

Where do most Puerto Ricans in the United States live?

Nearly a million Puerto Ricans live in New York City alone. That means the Big Apple has a bigger Puerto Rican population than San Juan, Puerto Rico's capital. Other places with growing populations of Puerto Ricans include Texas, Illinois, and Florida. Most Puerto Ricans on the mainland live in cities, but some are migrant farm workers who harvest potatoes and other produce in places like New York, New Jersey, and Connecticut.

What is a Nuyorican?

Nuyorican (or **Neorican**) is Spanglish for a Puerto Rican New Yorker. (Spanglish is an informal mix of English and Spanish, spoken by many Latinos.) Some Puerto

Even rain can't dampen the enthusiasm of these onlookers at New York City's annual Puerto Rican Day parade.

Ricans, however, object to the term. Puerto Ricans have their own names for certain sections of the city. East Harlem, or Spanish Harlem, has been a Puerto Rican enclave since the 1930s. Puerto Ricans call it El Barrio, or "the Neighborhood." The marketplace on Park Avenue in El Barrio is called La Marqueta. The Lower East Side, home to many Puerto Ricans, is known as Loisaida.

Do all Puerto Ricans stay in the United States once they're here?

No. Because they are U.S. citizens, they can easily migrate back and forth between island and mainland. Many do: in some years, the number of Puerto Ricans returning to the island has been greater than the number migrating to the mainland. Sometimes they are following jobs; sometimes they simply miss their family or the island culture.

The frequent traffic in both directions helps tie the two cultures together. Many people in the commonwealth speak English as well as Spanish. Those born on the mainland are regularly exposed to people from the commonwealth.

Are all Puerto Ricans blue-collar workers?

No, but a majority are. They work in the garment industry and in factories, hotels, and restaurants. Unemployment is high, thanks in large part to the flight of low-skilled manufacturing jobs from New York City over the last few decades. Lack of education, broken families, scarce housing, drugs, and crime are daily facts of life for the poorest Puerto Ricans.

However, the number of Puerto Ricans in white-collar professional and technical jobs is growing. As with many other groups originating from outside the United States, second-generation Puerto Ricans tend to have more education and do better financially than their parents.

Are Puerto Ricans black or white?

This is a variation on the old question, "Are Hispanics a race?" (see the chapter Who Are Hispanic Americans?). In the case of Puerto Ricans, the answer might be "neither," "both," or "the question is meaningless."

Hostos Community College in the Bronx, a borough of New York City, is named for Puerto Rican patriot and educator Eugenio María de Hostos (1839–1903).

The first Puerto Rican to serve in the U.S. Congress was Herman Badillo (1929–), a Puerto Rico-born Democrat who was elected to Congress from New York in 1970. In 1976, he cofounded the Congressional Hispanic Caucus.

Puerto Rico lacks the hard-and-fast separation between the races that is so much a part of life in the United States. Almost everyone in the commonwealth has some African and Native American mixed in with Spanish. There are not two races, but one ethnic culture with many racial gradations.

Most Puerto Ricans are **trigueño**, meaning they have light-brown skin. Lighter-skinned individuals are called **blanco**, or "white." Darker-skinned persons are **de color**, "of color." An **indio** is someone who looks Native American; a **moreno** looks like a black African. The terms **negro** or **negrito** are usually terms of endearment for people of any shade.

These racial groups intermarry, live in the same neighborhoods, and crop up in the same family. A brother may be *trigueño*, his sister *blanca*, their mother *de color*. Light-skinned people with European features more often occupy positions of high social rank than dark-skinned people. But high rank is not closed to dark-skinned people.

Puerto Ricans in the United States have had to cope with a starkly biracial, or two-race, system that wants to classify them as either black or white. Like Chicanos, Puerto Ricans sometimes refer to themselves as brown to signify that they are neither.

Who were the Young Lords?

The Young Lords were a Puerto Rican student activist group in New York City in the 1960s. Through protests and demonstrations, they forced the city to pay attention to the educational needs of young Puerto Ricans. They forced a shutdown of the City University of New York in 1969. They helped bring about the creation of Puerto Rican studies programs and student organizations at various colleges.

Was *West Side Story* based on real life?

The 1957 Broadway musical by Leonard Bernstein and Stephen Sondheim was ultimately based on Shakespeare's *Romeo and Juliet*. The creators of the show wanted to update that tragic love story by placing it in modern urban surroundings. They needed two warring camps, and originally thought of pitting Catholics against Jews. But by the

Se Habla Español

About 24 percent of New York City's 7.3 million people are of Hispanic descent—and Puerto Ricans are the single largest segment of those Hispanics. With those kinds of numbers, New York Puerto Ricans have an important say in how the city is run. They have been represented locally by numerous political figures of Puerto Rican ancestry, including Bronx borough president Fernando Ferrer, U.S. congressman José Serrano, labor leader Dennis Rivera, and onetime New York schools chancellor Joseph A. Fernández.

Perhaps the most visible sign of the Puerto Rican presence in the Big Apple is the heavy use of Spanish on signs, billboards, and public notices. Some Anglo straphangers get their first Spanish lessons reading subway ads for community health services and flights to Puerto Rico. The phrase *Se habla Español*—"Spanish spoken here"—can be found in many shop windows. In neighborhoods where Spanish prevails, "English spoken here" can even be spotted.

mid-1950s, the Puerto Rican migration to New York City gave them a better idea.

On Manhattan's West Side, Puerto Rican youths were running into Anglo teenage gangs who considered the newcomers a threat to their turf. The resulting gang warfare was immortalized in the Sharks, who were Puerto Rican, and the Jets, who were Anglo, in *West Side Story.*

The successful stage musical became a hit movie in 1961. Unfortunately for Puerto Ricans, the show stereotyped them as knife-wielding gang members, an image that still plagues them. One bright spot: *West Side Story* made a Broadway star of Chita Rivera, who played Anita, girlfriend of Sharks leader Bernardo. Puerto Rican by descent, Rivera was born in Washington, D.C., in 1933.

Were any of the leading Puerto Rican characters in the movie *West Side Story* actually played by Puerto Ricans?

Only one—Rita Moreno, who played the fiery Anita in the 1961 movie. Natalie Wood, who played the ill-fated lover Maria, was an American of Russian-French descent. George Chakiris, who played Maria's gang-leading brother Bernardo, was a Greek American.

Sweeping the Awards

The first performer ever to win an Oscar, a Tony, an Emmy, and a Grammy was Rita Moreno, a Puerto Rican.

The actress and singer was born Rosa Dolores Alverio in Humacao, Puerto Rico, in 1931. She moved to Manhattan as a child. She first appeared on Broadway at age thirteen and in movies at age fourteen. An enduring musical star of film, stage, and television, she won all four of the highest entertainment awards. She received an Oscar for best supporting actress in *West Side Story* (1962). She won a Tony for her stage appearance in *The Ritz* (1975). She was awarded two Emmys—for TV guest appearances on *The Muppet Show* in 1977 and *The Rockford Files* in 1978. She won a Grammy in 1972 for music from the children's TV series *The Electric Company*.

What was "Menuditis"?

This was the affliction of millions of teenage female fans of the Puerto Rican musical group Menudo. In the early 1980s, this band of five young male rock singers became all the rage among Hispanics in the United States and throughout the Western Hemisphere. Latina girls in love with the cute singers wore "I Love Menudo" buttons and bought Menudo T-shirts, boots, hats, and key chains. At concerts, Latinas screamed, moaned, and fainted.

Menuditis was the Hispanic equivalent of Beatlemania in the 1960s. Some Anglos began to enjoy their music as well, but it was Latinos—especially Puerto Ricans—who really created the Menudo phenomenon.

What is salsa?

This dance music, a variety of what is called Latin jazz, is a blend of Afro-Caribbean and Spanish influences and American jazz. It is popular among Anglos and Latinos alike. The name comes from *salsa picante*, or "hot sauce."

Salsa's greatest pioneer was Tito Puente (1930–), a New York–born bandleader and composer of Puerto Rican ancestry. Known as El Rey, or "the King," he began in the 1940s to bring Latin rhythms to both the popular dance-hall and elite jazz-concert circuits. Santana's 1970 rock hit "Oye Como Va" is a reinterpretation of a Puente composition.

Other Puerto Rican composers include Rafael Hernández, whose works such as "Lamento Borincano" incorporate Puerto Rican folk rhythms.

Who was the first major Puerto Rican TV star?

It was Freddie Prinze, who became famous for playing Chicano garage assistant Chico Rodriguez on *Chico and the Man* (1974–1978). The son of a Puerto Rican mother and a Hungarian father, Prinze joked that he was "Hungarican." While barely out of high school, he rocketed to fame as a stand-up comic and TV performer. Unable to bear the pressure of his sudden success, Prinze killed himself in 1977 at age twenty-two.

Who wrote *Down These Mean Streets*?

This gripping 1967 autobiography by Piri Thomas found a wide audience and is still read. Written in English but laced with street Spanish, it tells the story of the author's rough childhood in Spanish Harlem and the prison term he served for armed robbery. Other Puerto Rican writers include Jesús Colon, Miguel Algarin, and playwright René Marques.

Who was the first Latino to be named to the Baseball Hall of Fame?

It was Roberto Clemente, perhaps the best known of all Puerto Rican athletes. Born in Puerto Rico in 1934, he played for the Pittsburgh Pirates for eighteen seasons, from 1955 to 1972. With a lifetime batting average of .317, he was the first Latino to reach three thousand hits. He was considered the greatest defensive outfielder of his day and helped open the door to other Hispanic baseball players. He was also a humanitarian who worked for causes important to Puerto Ricans. His life was cut short in a plane crash in 1972. The plane had been carrying relief supplies to victims of an earthquake in Managua, Nicaragua.

It is no surprise that Puerto Rico should have produced a baseball player as great as Clemente. Baseball is Puerto Rico's national sport.

The work of Puerto Rican artists such as John Sanchez is showcased at El Museo del Barrio, a New York City art museum devoted to Latino art. Sanchez treats the theme of Puerto Rican independence in mixed-media works.

Poet William Carlos Williams (1883–1963) was the child of a Puerto Rican mother and an English father.

The figure of the jíbaro, *or farm worker, is regarded in Puerto Rican culture in much the same way as the cowboy in American culture —though he can also be mocked by modern urban Puerto Ricans as a "hick."*

One of the biggest religious holidays for Puerto Ricans is the Fiesta del Apóstol Santiago on July 25, which honors James the Apostle with music, dancing, and traditional costumes.

Why do people wear straw hats at the Puerto Rican Day Parade?

The annual Puerto Rican Day parade in June is one of New York City's biggest public events. (Similar parades are held in other northeastern cities.) It is a day of festivity and ethnic celebration, as bands, floats, and dancers in traditional costumes proceed past cheering crowds. The red, white, and blue Puerto Rican flag, with its lone star on a triangular field, waves everywhere. And many people wear a straw hat called a **pava**, the traditional hat of Puerto Rican farmers.

Are all Puerto Ricans Catholic?

The vast majority are, though a minority are Protestant. The biggest Protestant denomination is the Pentecostal Church of God. Many Puerto Ricans practice **Santería**, a Cuban-based blend of Catholic and West African elements (see the chapter Coming from Cuba). Stores called **botánicas** sell charms, incense, candles, herbs, and other paraphernalia related to Santería. *Botánicas* are as much a part of Puerto Rican neighborhoods as **bodegas**, the small mom-and-pop grocery stores familiar to urbanites, whether Latino or Anglo.

Democrat Fernando Ferrer has been elected the Bronx borough president for four consecutive terms and has used his position to bring housing and economic opportunity to this once rundown section of New York City. He is also prominent in national Hispanic politics: he hosted national presidential debates for Democratic Party candidates in 1988 and 1992 and was chairman of the Democratic National Committee's Hispanic Caucus.

Where Are All the Puerto Rican Restaurants?

Mexican, Cuban, and Spanish food can all be found on the menus of swanky restaurants, but Puerto Rican food rarely. This is true even in New York, where many Puerto Ricans have lived for decades. One can find Puerto Rican food in places serving **cuchifritos**, or fried pork entrails, to working-class people, but not in midtown fine-dining establishments. Why?

In *Latinos: A Biography of the People*, Earl Shorris claims the reason lies in the prejudices of middle-class Anglo customers. When Anglos dine out, says Shorris, they want not just food but symbols. Mexican food symbolizes the conquest and settlement of the great Southwest. Spain and Cuba are viewed as essentially European countries, linking the diner to the European past. But Puerto Rico symbolizes poverty and an unwanted racial mixture. "Puerto Ricans can't sell their food to Anglos at any price," he says.

What do Puerto Ricans eat?

Puerto Rican cuisine shares much in common with the island's Caribbean neighbors, Cuba and the Dominican Republic. The **comidas criollas**—or Creole foods—of all these island nations include beans and rice (**Moros y Christianos**, or "Moors and Christians"), roast suckling pig (or **lechón**), the **plantain** (a cooking banana), and the **yuca** (a starchy root vegetable). **Flan**, a custard, is often served as dessert, and rum is the preferred drink. But Puerto Ricans also have distinctive dishes: **mofongo**, which combines plantains, beans, and pork; the chicken and rice dish called **asopao**; the boiled pies called **pasteles**; and **sofrito**, a seasoning paste. **Cuchifritos**, or fried pork entrails, are a snack.

Which is closer to Florida: Cuba or Washington, D.C.? ◆ How many people live in Cuba? ◆ Why is Cuba called the Pearl of the Antilles? ◆ Are most Cubans black or white? ◆ Why did Cuba become independent of Spain at the same time as most of Latin America? ◆ Did the United States ever try to annex Cuba? ◆ Who was José Martí? ◆ Were there real Spanish atrocities in the Cuban War of Independence? ◆ What does the phrase "Remember the Maine!" have to do with Cuba? ◆ Was it the newspapers that forced the United States into the Spanish-American War? Who won the Spanish-American War? ◆ What was the

COMING FROM CUBA

Which is closer to Florida: Cuba or Washington, D.C.?

Cuba, the largest island in the West Indies, is only ninety miles from Key West, Florida. By contrast, the U.S. capital of Washington is more than seven hundred miles from the nearest large Florida city, Jacksonville. The closeness of Cuba to the United States has made it an object of American interest from the days when it still belonged to Spain. The closeness has also made it possible for Cuban immigrants to come to the United States.

How many people live in Cuba?

About 11 million. In addition, nearly one million people of Cuban descent live in the United States. More than 700,000 of these are immigrants. They came to the United States since communist dictator Fidel Castro took power in 1959. Most of them are vigorously opposed to Castro's regime.

Why is Cuba called the Pearl of the Antilles?

Christopher Columbus, who discovered Cuba on his first voyage in 1492, described it as "the fairest island human eyes have yet beheld." Lush with trees and fresh water, Cuba is as big as Pennsylvania (about 43,000 square miles). The climate is balmy but not sweltering. There are some mountains, but most of the land is flat and fertile, with many good harbors for ships.

Colonized from 1511, Cuba also proved to have strategic value. Lying at the entrance to the Gulf of Mexico and bordering the Caribbean Sea, it served the Spanish as a base for expeditions to the whole region, including Mexico and Florida. The Spanish soon extermi- nated Cuba's native Taino and Ciboney, but other workers were readily found: African slaves. By the early nine- teenth century, the colony's masters were prospering on exports of sugar, coffee, and tobacco. As the most pre- cious jewel in the island groups known as the Greater and Lesser Antilles, Cuba earned the nickname "Pearl of the Antilles."

Are most Cubans black or white?

About 66 percent of the islanders are categorized as white, descended from Spanish colonists. Twenty-two per- cent are a mix of white and black, combining Spanish and African ancestry. Twelve percent are black. Because Native Americans were wiped out early in the conquest, they are not a major racial component.

The distinctions between races has been more impor- tant in Cuba than in Puerto Rico. In Puerto Rico almost everyone acknowledges some racial mixing. In Cuba, the majority take pride in claiming unmixed white ancestry.

Racism in Cuba was never as severe as in the United States. Even during slavery (abolished in 1886), African slaves had the right to buy their freedom. Mulattoes, chil- dren of black and white couples, were given many of the privileges of whites. Still, there was a color line. In colonial times as in the years of independence before Castro's revo- lution, white people were more likely to occupy the upper and middle classes than blacks.

In 1971, Cuban leader Fidel Castro pro- claimed, "We are not only a Latin American nation; we are an Afro- American nation also."

Why didn't Cuba become independent of Spain at the same time as most of Latin America?

As in Puerto Rico, many people in Cuba at first felt too dependent on Spain to risk fighting for independence. Who would buy the sugar or protect the security of such a small nation? Cuba and Puerto Rico remained loyal to Spain even in the 1820s, when Spain's other American colonies finished winning their independence.

But, as in Puerto Rico, a movement for independence gained momentum. As Cuban patriots called for more autonomy, Spain became more repressive, banning political meetings and raising taxes and tariffs. In 1868, Cuban rebels in the town of Yara declared independence in what was called El Grito de Yara, "the Cry of Yara." It was the beginning of a long, doomed war for independence known as the Ten Years' War. Spain harshly suppressed the revolt; about 200,000 people died. By 1878, the war was over, and Cuba was still a colony.

Did the United States ever try to annex Cuba?

Early in the nineteenth century, several prominent Americans were eager to lay hands on the rich Spanish colony so close to U.S. shores. In 1809 Thomas Jefferson said, "We must have Cuba." In 1823, Secretary of State John Quincy Adams argued that annexation of Cuba was "indispensable" to America's "continuance and integrity." In 1848, President James K. Polk went so far as to offer Spain $100 million for Cuba. Spain angrily turned down the offer, saying they would rather see the island "sink into the ocean" than become part of the United States. Even so, interest in acquiring Cuba continued until 1898, when the Spanish American War made it a real possibility.

Who was José Martí?

José Martí (1853–1895) was a poet, journalist, and the greatest hero of the Cuban struggle for independence. He was arrested for his revolutionary activities at age sixteen. After his release, he spent much of his life in exile, some of it in the United States. He founded and led the Cuban Revolutionary Party and wrote about the type of republic he sought. He envisioned an independent Cuba with social justice and political liberty.

In 1895, a new rebellion broke out in Cuba. Martí returned from New York City to lead the fighting. He was killed in the battle of Dos Ríos, but the Cuban War of Independence (1895–1898) continued.

Were there really Spanish atrocities in the Cuban War of Independence?

You will often read in history books that Americans were outraged by news reports of Spanish atrocities, or cruel actions, in the Cuban War of Independence. Some of the atrocities were real. Cuban civilians were herded into concentration camps, where about 100,000 died of disease, hunger, and mistreatment. But some of the atrocities were exaggerated to boost the circulation of U.S. newspapers. News magnates William Randolph Hearst and Joseph Pulitzer, fighting each other for circulation, found that the war made good press. When they demanded that the United States join the war on the side of the rebels, many Americans concurred—and bought more newspapers.

What does the phrase "Remember the *Maine!*" have to do with Cuba?

The *Maine* was a U.S. battleship that exploded in the harbor of Havana, Cuba's capital, on February 15, 1898.

This 1898 lithograph depicts the destruction of the U.S. battleship *Maine* in Havana Harbor, Cuba. Such illustrations in popular newspapers helped turn U.S. opinion toward war with Spain.

Who Blew Up the *Maine*?

The problem with the slogan "Remember the *Maine!*" was that no one knew for sure how the *Maine* blew up. Americans assumed that a Spanish mine had destroyed it, but the Spanish denied it. Indeed, Spain wanted very much to avoid war with the powerful United States, and tried to settle the dispute diplomatically after the explosion. Cuban rebels had no interest in getting the United States involved. They were already close to winning the war, and feared correctly that the United States would take over if it entered the fighting. Some have charged that the United States itself blew up the ship to create a pretext for war, though that is far-fetched. But it is possible no one blew up the *Maine*. The ammunition stored in the warship may have ignited spontaneously, causing the disaster.

Two hundred and sixty crew members died. Spain was accused of setting off the explosion, and American newspapers and people in the street trumpeted the battle cry, "Remember the *Maine!*" President William McKinley had previously been opposed to war. But he now found the pressure for war too great to stand. In April, the United States declared war on Spain.

Was it the newspapers that forced the United States into the Spanish American War?

Hardly. American presidents do not declare war because a few journalists tell them to do so. The pressure for war did not come merely from newspapers and outraged common people. U.S. businessmen had invested about $50 million in sugar plantations, railroads, mines, and other enterprises in Cuba. They wanted a greater U.S. presence on the island to protect and expand their investments. Meanwhile, American imperialists such as Senator Henry Cabot Lodge urged the building of an American overseas empire. Imperialists wanted overseas naval bases and a strong navy to allow U.S. commerce to expand abroad. The urgings of empire builders were at least as strong an influence on President McKinley as the popular wish to help Cubans achieve freedom.

*American secre-
tary of state
John Hay called
the Spanish
American War
"that splendid
little war."*

Who won the Spanish American War?

In what was called the Spanish-American War, the United States defeated Spain in about four months of fighting, from April to August 1898. Among the Americans who fought in the war was future president Theodore Roosevelt (1858–1919). He led his cavalry brigade of Rough Riders in a successful attack on Kettle Hill (not, as it is sometimes called, San Juan Hill).

As a result of the war, Puerto Rico, Guam, and the Philippines became U.S. territories, and Spain renounced its claim to Cuba. The United States had stated earlier that it would not annex Cuba, and it did not. But Cuba did not exactly become independent.

What was the Platt Amendment?

U.S. troops occupied Cuba until 1902. Before withdrawing the troops, the United States required the new nation of Cuba to agree to the Platt Amendment. This legislation was named for U.S. senator Orville Platt, who introduced it in Congress in 1901. The Platt Amendment said that the United States could intervene in Cuba at any time to maintain public order or the nation's independence. Cuba was forbidden to sign treaties that would give power over its affairs to countries other than the United States. The United States had the right to build naval bases on the island.

In other words, Cuba was independent in name, but not in reality. In reality, the United States could station troops in Cuba and use military force whenever some Cuban decision displeased it. On three separate occasions, in response to uprisings, the United States did send troops

Don Corleone's Cuba

In the movie *The Godfather, Part II* (1974), mob leader Michael Corleone (played by Al Pacino) comes to Batista-era Cuba to try to close a criminal deal. The scene is based on historical truth. Under Batista, Havana became a center for prostitution and drugs. Gambling casinos flourished, run by organized criminals from the United States.

to Cuba: 1906, 1912, and 1917. Throughout the early twentieth century, U.S. investment on the island increased until the sugar industry and most other businesses were under American control.

Thousands of Cubans had died to win independence. No wonder Cubans hated the Platt Amendment and the U.S. domination it represented. In 1934, the Platt Amendment was repealed, but the damage had been done. Cuba was, in effect, an American colony.

Which Cuban leader was born poorer, Fulgencio Batista or Fidel Castro?

Fulgencio Batista y Zaldívar (1901–1973) was a Cuban dictator whose regime was famous for its corruption, its support by rich Cubans, and its strong ties to the United States. Fidel Castro Ruz (1926–) was the revolutionary who overthrew him on behalf of Cuba's poor and downtrodden. But only one of the two was born poor, and it wasn't Castro.

Batista was born to a lower-class rural family of mixed Spanish and African descent. He rose through the army ranks and helped overthrow the dictator Gerardo Machado in 1933. From 1933 to 1958, as head of the army, Batista dominated Cuban politics. From 1952, he governed as an outright dictator. He repressed opponents ruthlessly and freely pocketed public money. Under his rule, the gulf between rich and poor grew.

Unlike Batista, Castro was the son of a wealthy plantation owner. Of Spanish descent, he received a law degree from the University of Havana. Instead of being faithful to his social class, Castro was faithful to his ideals. He wanted to free Cuba from U.S. domination and relieve the sufferings of the poor. To do so, he believed he had to overthrow Batista.

Why do people in Cuba celebrate July 26?

This was the day in 1953 when Castro launched his first attack on the Batista regime, at the Moncada army base. Outnumbered ten to one, Castro's forces failed and he was arrested. He was sent into exile in Mexico, but he was soon back to try again.

From 1956 to 1959, in what is called the Cuban revolution, Castro and his troops waged guerrilla warfare from their base in Cuba's Sierra Maestra. They raided army posts and blew up property. Peasant farmers shielded them and volunteered as soldiers, viewing Castro as their best hope for a better life. Castro's top officers included his brother Raúl Castro and Che Guevara. The rebels called themselves the Twenty-sixth of July Movement, in honor of Castro's first daring blow.

Was Che Guevara Cuban?

No. Ernesto "Che" Guevara (1928–1967) was a former medical student from Argentina who dedicated his life to fighting in revolutionary wars in Latin America and Africa. He was Fidel Castro's chief lieutenant in the Cuban revolution (1956–1959) and minister of industry afterward (1961–1965). An expert in guerrilla warfare, he left Cuba so he could carry on the struggle in other oppressed nations. He was executed in Bolivia and was revered as a hero and martyr throughout the Third World. (The Third World is a name for the impoverished former colonies of Europe in Latin America, Africa, and Asia.) His portrait, with beret and scruffy beard, inspired left-wing protesters even in the United States.

When did Castro win?

Fittingly, on New Year's Day. In the early hours of January 1, 1959, Batista realized his days were numbered and fled Cuba by plane. A few days later, Castro's troops marched victoriously into Havana.

Why didn't the United States like Castro?

The U.S. government feared from the beginning that Castro was a communist, even though he said at first that he wasn't. He nationalized private businesses, including U.S.-owned industries and plantations. This meant he took them as property of the state—without paying the previous owners for what he had taken. He executed or imprisoned opponents on the island. He asked the U.S. government for economic aid. When the United States refused, he formed an alliance with the Soviet Union, the principal adversary

What Is Communism?

As developed by German philosopher Karl Marx and Russian revolutionary Vladimir Ilich Lenin, communism is a political system that seeks to combat poverty and injustice. Unlike capitalists, who believe in private enterprise, communists believe that the state should control economic life by owning and managing all or most industries. Unlike liberal democrats, communists believe the state should be ruled by a small Communist Party elite. Opposition to the rulers should be suppressed. Marxist-Leninists do not believe in God and think religion should be discouraged. Instead, all citizens should be instructed in Communist doctrine.

Communism is a form of socialism, the belief that the government should control some aspects of economic life for the good of the people as a whole. But socialists are not necessarily opposed to religion or democratic government. Marxist-Leninist communists are.

In the Russian Revolution of 1917, the Union of Soviet Socialist Republics, or Soviet Union, was born.

It was the world's first nation founded on communist principles. By 1959, it had become very powerful—the only superpower besides the United States. It controlled the nations of eastern Europe and was allied to communist China.

The United States government was bitterly opposed to communism, which many Americans felt endangered their way of life. Because both the United States and Soviet Union had nuclear weapons that could destroy the world, they feared going to war with each other. Instead, the Soviet Union and the United States were locked in a Cold War. Through allied and puppet governments, each struggled to keep the other from extending its field of influence—for example, in Cuba. Each built up huge military arsenals in preparation for a war they hoped would never come.

In 1991, the Soviet Union collapsed, ending the Cold War. Its major component, Russia, became a democratic, capitalist nation. Communism was not dead: it survives in China and Cuba. But its greatest champion had died.

of the United States. In 1961, he openly avowed that he was a Marxist-Leninist. By then, the United States had already broken off diplomatic relations with Cuba. The United States banned travel or trade between the countries—a ban that still stands, although restrictions were eased in 1998.

Cuba's infant mortality rate is a relatively low 8 in 1,000. In the nearby Dominican Republic, a country friendly to the United States, the rate is 46 in 1,000.

Did any of Cuba remain in U.S. hands after Castro took over?

Yes. In 1903, the United States established a naval base at Guantánamo Bay in southeastern Cuba. Protected by treaty, the base has stayed in operation ever since—despite pressure from Castro to give it up. It is located in the province of Guantánamo, homeland of the farm girl in the Cuban folk ballad "Guantánamera"—which, oddly, became a hit in the United States.

How many people left Cuba right after the Castro revolution?

From 1959 to 1962, about 155,000 people fled Cuba for the United States. Some were Batistianos—rich allies of Batista. Known as "golden exiles," they brought along the fortunes they had made from his corrupt regime. Some were wealthy people whose ranches, plantations, or industries had been nationalized. Many were professionals who were considered a little too prosperous: doctors, lawyers, judges, bankers. And many were middle-class people who were also targets of Castro: office workers, teachers, and civil servants.

The peasants who were the vast majority of Cubans were less inclined to leave. Castro lowered food prices and redistributed land to benefit farm workers. He gave every Cuban access to medical care. He established schools so that Cuba's literacy rate is now 94 percent, the highest in Latin America.

As a communist and atheist, Fidel Castro was a staunch opponent of the Catholic Church. But the young Castro had been educated by Jesuits in Catholic schools. In 1998 Castro allowed Pope John Paul II to visit Cuba and speak to the people.

Why do we speak of "Cuban exiles" instead of "Cuban immigrants"?

People who left Castro's Cuba for the United States prefer to call themselves exiles. This term implies that they came to this country not for economic improvement, like most immigrants, but to flee political tyranny. It also expresses their early hope that they would return to Cuba once Castro fell from power. In Cuba, exiles are known by a different term: **gusanos,** or "worms," who abandoned the revolution.

Were there Cubans in the United States before the Castro revolution?

Yes. The United States was a haven for Cuban exiles even during Spanish colonial times. About five thousand

Cubans, including many who fought for Cuban independence in the Ten Years' War, found refuge in the United
States in the late nineteenth century. Once Cuba achieved
independence in 1902, Cubans continued to come to the
United States, fleeing political instability at home.

Why didn't the United States just overthrow Castro's regime?

The United States tried. On April 17, 1961, an invasion
force of about 1,500 Cuban exiles landed in the Bay of
Pigs, Cuba. They were supported by the United States—
but not very well. The Central Intelligence Agency (CIA)
had promised the exiles full-scale U.S. military support,
but President John F. Kennedy withdrew it at the last
minute. The invaders were left unprotected to face
Castro's vastly more powerful armed forces, which killed
about 120 and took nearly 1,200 prisoner. CIA reports that
ordinary Cubans would rise up to join the invaders were
dead wrong.

The Bay of Pigs was a fiasco that embarrassed
the United States and delighted Castro. Cuban exiles felt
betrayed by the Democratic president. Ever since they

President John F.
Kennedy and his
wife Jacqueline
greet Cuban
exiles gathered in
Miami Stadium on
December 29, 1962.
The Kennedy
Admistration's mis-
handling of the
Bay of Pigs invasion
alienated many
Cuban Americans
from the Demo-
cratic Party.

started becoming U.S. citizens, they have voted solidly Republican. A few have even engaged in bombings and other terrorist acts intended to draw attention to their cause.

What was the Cuban Missile Crisis?

Kennedy flinched from a full-scale invasion of Cuba because he feared a nuclear showdown with the Soviet Union. Perceiving Kennedy as weak, the Soviet Union forced that showdown only eighteen months later—in the Cuban Missile Crisis.

In October 1962, U.S. spy planes reported that the Soviet Union was assembling nuclear missile sites in Cuba. Kennedy ordered a naval blockade of Cuba and prepared to invade the island unless the Soviet Union accepted his demand to dismantle the missile sites. For two weeks, the world hovered on the brink of a catastrophic nuclear war. Then the Soviet Union accepted Kennedy's demand.

It was clear after the Cuban Missile Crisis that the United States would not be invading Cuba any time soon. The risk of nuclear war was too great. Cuban exiles settled in for a long, perhaps permanent, stay in the United States.

How did the fall of the Soviet Union affect Cuba?

It hurt Castro's government drastically. For decades, the Soviet Union had been Cuba's principal source of arms, trade, and economic assistance. Since the Soviet Union collapsed in 1991, Cuba's economic situation has been dire. Cuban exiles are waiting eagerly for Castro's government to collapse or for Castro to die of old age. They hope that communism will be abolished and free trade and travel between the countries will resume.

Marxist-Leninist Cuba staggers along. Its main trading partners today are Argentina, Bulgaria, China, and the countries of the former Soviet Union. About 75 percent of its exports are sugar or sugar products.

How did Cuban exiles do in the United States?

On the whole, they did very well—better than any other Hispanic American group. They were helped by the U.S. government, which welcomed them as refugees from

Coke Is It

One of the greatest Cuban American success stories is that of Roberto C. Guizeta (1931–1997). Born in Havana, he was educated at Yale and became a chemical engineer for Coca-Cola in Cuba. He fled Castro's revolution in 1960. By 1981, he had risen to become the company's chairman and chief executive officer. He was credited with innovative changes that raised the total value of Coke's stock from $4 billion to $150 billion by the time of his death.

a communist regime, and therefore allies. Cuban exiles easily received permanent residency status. They got free temporary housing, medical care, financial aid, and job counseling.

But they also had to help themselves. Cubans who had been lawyers or accountants now found themselves washing dishes or cleaning bathrooms until they could find better jobs. Their life savings taken by Castro, they suffered hunger and humiliation. Still, as middle-class people with education and skills, they soon rose.

Cubans credit their success to a cultural quality of **atrevimiento** (daring or boldness). It didn't hurt that most were white. Anglo prejudice against Cubans was not as great as against racially mixed Mexicans and Puerto Ricans.

Where is Little Havana?

It is a Cuban American neighborhood in Miami, Florida. Here Spanish is widely spoken. Shops and restaurants reminiscent of Cuba line the main drag, Calle Ocho (Spanish for "eighth street"). Older men play dominoes, a favorite pastime of Cubans—not to mention their West Indian neighbors, Puerto Ricans and Dominicans. The existence of Little Havana is one sign of how Cubans have transformed Miami.

The change is mostly credited to the Cuban exiles, who settled in large numbers in Miami. The city is only 150 miles from Cuba and already had a small Cuban American population before the exiles arrived. Its warm climate and large Cuban population reminded them of the old country,

In the late 1950s, Miami had only about 46,000 people of Cuban descent. Today, more than 700,000 Cuban Americans live in Miami and the rest of Dade County.

la cuba de ayer ("Cuba of yesterday"), for which they felt nostalgia. Some resettled in other parts of the country, only to return to Miami.

How have Cuban Americans changed Miami?

When exiles from Castro's Cuba first arrived in Miami, it was a small, sleepy retirement town. Now it is a thriving metropolis, a center of international finance and trade with a population that is more than 60 percent Hispanic. It is a bilingual city with Spanish-language newspapers and radio and TV stations.

Much of Miami's commerce is with Latin America. In the 1960s, the countries of Latin America were increasing their trade with the United States. As Spanish-speaking, educated people with a knowledge of Latino culture, Cuban Americans were the perfect liaisons between the northern and southern Americas. They helped change Miami into a commercial gateway to Latin America.

Miami's first Cuban American mayor, Xavier L. Suárez, was elected in 1985.

Did Castro try to restrict emigration?

Not at first. But beginning in 1961, Castro put up barriers to emigration. For example, exiles were not allowed to take anything more than $5 in U.S. money and a few clothes. Emigration to the United States was banned from 1962 to 1965, and again beginning in 1973. In 1980, Castro decided to let some would-be emigrants go. Because these 125,000 refugees left by boat from the port of Mariel, they were called **Marielitos.**

Why did Marielitos get a bad name?

To many Americans of the early 1980s, Marielitos were considered a problem. They were not warmly embraced like the earlier Cuban exiles. They were usually not given the noble title exiles, but were called refugees.

Cuban Americans live in other places besides Miami. There are large Cuban American communities in Union City, New Jersey; Washington, D.C.; and New York City.

One reason is that the United States was in the midst of economic crisis at the time, and did not feel it could afford to help. To make matters worse, most Marielitos were poor. They lacked the professional skills and middle-class background that earlier Cuban exiles had displayed. Some Marielitos had criminal records or had been diagnosed as being mentally ill. In addition, many were of African descent, while most earlier Cuban refugees had been white. In a country with deep racism, this alone was enough to make them seem undesirable. Cuban Americans themselves sometimes snubbed Marielitos, afraid that Anglos would confuse the two groups.

Were all Marielitos criminals?

Not at all. The vast majority were law-abiding people. But a small number were convicted criminals whom Castro deported. Within a year, sixty-six Mariel refugees had been arrested for crimes in Miami. About 2,700 Marielitos were refused permission to enter the United States, whether for old criminal records, current crimes, or other reasons. Most of these people languished in prison for years, pawns in the feud between Castro and the United States. Marielito-led prison riots in 1987 forced the United States to pay attention to the detained Cubans. Their cases were heard individually. Some were allowed to stay in the United States, others sent back to Cuba.

Do Cubans still come to the United States?

Yes. Castro still forbids emigration, but Cubans find their way out: in boats by night; on rafts made of inner tubes; by way of Mexico or other countries. Baseball pitcher Livan Hernández defected to Mexico in 1995. Before long, he was playing for the Florida Marlins and helped the team win the 1997 World Series. Hernández was named most valuable player in the series and won another reward: Castro allowed the player's mother to leave Cuba to join him for the seventh game.

His younger half-brother Orlando Hernández, nick-named El Duque, was an outstanding pitcher on the Cuban National Team. A year after Livan defected, in October 1996 Orlando was banned from playing baseball in Cuba. On December 26, 1997, Orlando fled Cuba with a group of other Cubans. By spring 1998, he had been signed to a four-year $6.6 million contract by New York Yankees.

Have there been other Cuban baseball players?

There have been quite a few. Cuban American Tony Oliva, for example, was a star hitter and later coach for the

Bandleader Xavier Cugat (1900–1990), who helped intro-duce Latin music to American audiences in the 1930s, was born in Spain but raised in Cuba. He was married to Charo, a Latina singer, comedian, and frequent guest on Johnny Carson's The Tonight Show.

The Mambo Kings Play Songs of Love, *a 1989 novel by Cuban American Oscar Hijuelos (1951–), tells the story of two Cuban brothers who play music in New York City clubs. The novel won a Pulitzer Prize and was made into a movie,* The Mambo Kings *(1992).*

Radio Martí is an anticommunist American station beamed at Cuba since 1985. Established to support opponents of Castro, it is named for Cuban patriot José Martí, who is claimed as a revolutionary forefather by both Castro and his critics.

Minnesota Twins beginning in 1964. Other Cuban American ball players have included Preston Gomez, Mike González, and Vic Powers.

Was Desi Arnaz a refugee of Castro?

No. The Cuban-born musician and actor (1917–1986) came to the United States in the 1930s, fleeing Batista, not Castro. Arnaz married comedienne Lucille Ball and starred with her in the hit TV comedy "I Love Lucy" (1951–1957). Playing a bandleader in the show, Arnaz introduced millions of Americans to Afro-Cuban music, with its **bongo** drums and **maracas**. He also made it more possible for Americans to imagine a successful, middle-class person who happened to be Hispanic.

Did the rumba originate in Cuba?

Yes. The **rumba** is one of several dances and musical forms that originated in Latin America and became popular in the United States from the 1940s on. Afro-Cuban percussionist Chano Pozo played in the band of American jazz trumpeter Dizzy Gillespie's band, where Cuban rhythms blended with American bebop, a type of jazz. Cuban American singer Celia Cruz performed with Tito Puente, Puerto Rican king of salsa—a musical style that owes as much to Cuba as to Puerto Rico.

Cuban Americans are also found in the world of classical music and dance. They include pianist Horacio Gutiérrez and ballet dancer Fernando Bujones. In the pop music scene, no Cuban American performer has been more notable than Gloria Estefan. Singing in both English and Spanish, she and her Miami Sound Machine have sold millions of records among Latinos and Anglos alike.

How does a Cuban American girl celebrate her "coming out" into society?

Many Cuban American girls celebrate their fifteenth birthday with a **quince** (Spanish for "fifteen"). Similar to a debutante ball or a sweet sixteen bash, this elaborate party traditionally marks a girl as eligible for dating. Wealthy Cuban Americans may spend more money on a *quince* than many people spend on weddings. The practice has spread to some other Latino communities.

Cuban Cigars

The most prized cigars in the world come from Cuba—perhaps because Cubans invented cigars. The Taino and Ciboney people of Cuba were growing tobacco and rolling the leaves into cigars before Columbus arrived. Cubans of Spanish descent made a lucrative industry out of the Native American practice. Today, cigars are rolled in many countries, including the United States, where Cuban Americans in Key West and Tampa, Florida, have produced cigars since the nineteenth century. The Cuban cigar industry is important to Cuba's economy, but increasing knowledge about the dangers of tobacco has reduced the number of smokers. But many cigar aficionados still believe the most exquisite smoke comes from Cuba.

What is a santo?

To Spanish-speaking Roman Catholics, a **santo** is a saint. To devotees of the religion called Santería, it is something more: an **orishá**, a spirit or god who can procure material benefits for believers. Santería originated with West African slaves, who brought their Yoruba religion to Cuba and blended it with Catholic beliefs. A *santo* is both a saint—such as Saint Peter—and a Yoruba deity such as Ogun, patron of miners and workers. The *santos* are worshiped through animal sacrifice and food-sharing rituals. For help with specific life problems, charms and potions are available.

Most Cuban Americans are strictly Roman Catholic, but some follow Santería. So do some people from Puerto Rico, Venezuela, and elsewhere in Latin America. Desi Arnaz's signature song "Babaloo" was originally a hymn to the *santo* Babalú.

What is *ropa vieja*?

Ropa vieja is a Cuban stew of shredded beef; the name means "old clothes." Cubans also enjoy many of the same comidas criollas as other West Indian Latinos: roast pig, plantains, rice and beans (preferably black beans). A **boniato** is something like a stuffed, deep-fried potato; **arroz moro** is a beans and rice dish. A Cuban sandwich is a pressed and toasted assortment of foods.

A cafecita is a variety of espresso, or strong black coffee, in a small cup. It is also known as cafe cubano, or Cuban coffee. If you can't get to Cuba, you can enjoy a cafecita at cafés in Miami, or perhaps a batido, or tropical milk-shake.

Why are there Cuban Chinese restaurants?

Cuban Chinese restaurants, readily found in cities with large Cuban American populations, blend the two cuisines. They exist because a minority of Cubans are people of Chinese descent. More than 100,000 Chinese contract workers came to Cuba between 1840 and 1870, at a time when African slave labor was being phased out.

What does it mean to call someone a YUCA?

Playing on the Caribbean food named yuca, a **YUCA** is a young, upwardly mobile, Cuban American—in other words, a Cuban yuppie. These are people in their thirties (or slightly older) who came from Cuba as small children or were born in the United States. They are well-educated, have successful careers, and tend to be more liberal than their parents. They can speak both English and Spanish, but prefer English and have little interest in living in Cuba should the Castro regime fall. Their children have even less interest in doing so.

How many Dominican Americans are there in the United States? ◆ Where is the Dominican Republic? ◆ What in the rest of Hispaniola? ◆ Why are people from the Dominican Republic usually lighter-skinned than people from Haiti? ◆ Did the United States ever send troops to the Dominican Republic? ◆ Who was Rafael Trujillo ◆ How did Trujillo come to power? ◆ What happened after Trujillo was killed? ◆ Have conditions in the Dominican Republic improved in recent years? ◆ When did Dominicans start coming in larger numbers to the United States? ◆ How do undocumented immigrant from the Dominican Republic get to the United States

COMING FROM THE DOMINICAN REPUBLIC

How many Dominican Americans are there in the United States?

The 1990 census counted 506,000, but the real number today is probably close to a million. In other words, there are about as many Dominican Americans as there are Cuban Americans. It is hard to know the exact number because many Dominican immigrants have come to the country illegally. Those who do so live in danger of deportation if caught. The economic situation in their own country, the Dominican Republic, is so bad that they keep coming.

Where is the Dominican Republic?

The Dominican Republic occupies the eastern two-thirds of the Caribbean island of Hispaniola. The island is sandwiched between Cuba to the west and Puerto Rico to the east. At about 19,000 square miles in area, the Dominican Republic is a little smaller than West Virginia but much more densely populated, with about 8 million people. Two million live in the capital, Santo Domingo, named for Spain's Saint Dominic.

What's in the rest of Hispaniola?

The western third of the mountainous island is occupied by Haiti. Back in the seventeenth century, France colonized

Founded by Christopher Columbus in 1496, Santo Domingo is the oldest surviving city of European origin in the Americas. Some say Columbus's bones still rest there.

the western part of Hispaniola while Spain was busy with the eastern part. The French part was called Saint-Domingue, the Spanish part Santo Domingo. Spain officially ceded the western part to France in 1697. In 1795, having done little to develop the colony, Spain gave up the eastern part as well.

In 1804, Saint-Domingue became the independent nation of Haiti (from the Arawak name meaning "land of mountains"). It was only the second nation in the Americas to win independence, after the United States.

At the time, Santo Domingo was part of Haiti. But the cultures were so different—one rooted in France, the other in Spain—that Dominicans craved to be free of Haiti. On the other hand, they weren't sure if they wanted to be independent or a colony of Spain. They were reconquered by Spain (1809–1821), briefly independent (1821–1822), then reconquered by Haiti (1822–1844). Finally, in 1844, the independent Dominican Republic was founded. Except for a few years of Spanish rule (1861–1865), it has remained independent since, with Haiti as its next-door neighbor.

Why are people from the Dominican Republic usually lighter-skinned than people from Haiti?

The two different colonial regimes—French and Spanish—produced a different racial picture in the two halves of Hispaniola. Both colonies employed black slave labor from Africa. But French colonists were more likely to keep the races segregated than Spanish colonists. Today, about 95 percent of Haitians are direct descendants of African slaves; most of the rest are mulattoes, a mix of white and black. In the Dominican Republic, almost everyone is mulatto, with only a small minority claiming pure white or pure black ancestry.

Did the United States ever send troops to the Dominican Republic?

Yes—more than once. Political turmoil, corruption, and civil war have plagued the country since its founding. In 1869, things were so bad that the Dominican Republic's president negotiated a treaty in which the United States would annex the country. The U.S. Senate refused to ratify

Roosevelt's Corollary

In 1823, U.S. president James Monroe stated his Monroe Doctrine. It was issued at a time when most of Latin America had just become independent. Monroe's foreign policy statement warned that the United States would not tolerate new colonization of the Americas by European powers. In years to come, it came to mean something more: that the United States had the right to reign supreme over Latin America. President Theodore Roosevelt made this position explicit with his Roosevelt Corollary of 1904. It inferred from the Monroe Doctrine that the United States had a duty at times to intervene in Latin American affairs:

> Chronic wrongdoing, or an impotence which results in a general loosening of ties of civilized society... may force the United States, however, reluctantly, in flagrant cases of such wrongdoing or impotence, to the exercise of an international police power.

Not surprisingly, Latin Americans viewed both the Monroe Doctrine and the Roosevelt Corollary with distaste and alarm. Too often, these principles seemed like thin disguises for a policy of "might makes right."

---

the treaty. But in 1905, U.S. president Theodore Roosevelt began a long period of active American involvement in Dominican affairs. The Dominican Republic's finances were near collapse, in part because government officials were pocketing customs money. European creditors were threatening to intervene forcibly if debts were not paid. To prevent this from happening, Roosevelt arranged for the United States to administer the country's customs department. He was applying his Roosevelt Corollary to the Monroe Doctrine, which, in essence, allowed the United States to intervene in Latin America whenever the president felt U.S. interests were threatened.

This arrangement lasted until 1941. Civil disorders continued, and the United States sent in the marines. From 1916 to 1924, the marines occupied the country. During that time, U.S. investment on the island greatly increased, and most of the sugar-growing land passed into American hands.

The next time U.S. troops came to the Dominican Republic was in 1965, during the political chaos that followed the assassination of dictator Rafael Trujillo (1891–1961).

Who was Rafael Trujillo?

Known as El Jefe, or "the Chief," he was the dictator of the Dominican Republic from 1930 to 1961. He wasn't always president, but he controlled whoever was president. He ruled like a gangster, outlawing opposition parties, torturing and killing dissidents, growing rich on public money. He expanded the economy and modernized the country, but ordinary citizens did not benefit much: unemployment and poverty were rampant. In a dispute with Haiti, Trujillo ordered the massacre of ten thousand Haitians. He was shot to death in his car by assassins in 1961. Many breathed a sigh of relief when his brutal reign came to an end.

How had Trujillo come to power?

He was trained by U.S. Marines during the occupation and backed by the United States during the early part of his reign. Later, the United States grew discontented with him. The CIA reportedly aided his assassination.

Rafael Trujillo waves to onlookers from the Plaza Hotel during a visit to New York City on February 22, 1953. Known and hated by many Dominicans for his brutal dictatorship, he was assassinated in 1961.

What happened after Trujillo was killed?

A few more years of turmoil followed. Opposition leader Juan Bosch was elected president in 1962, but deposed by a military coup the following year. Bosch's supporters rebelled in 1965—and the United States again sent in marines.

Although Bosch denied it, the United States considered Bosch's supporters to be communists. In the midst of the Cold War, the United States did not intend to "lose" the Dominican Republic to communism the way it had "lost" Cuba. With U.S. assistance, new elections were held in 1966. Joaquín Balaguer, a staunch anticommunist and former ally of El Jefe, was elected president. Reelected several times, he held the office until 1978 and again from 1986 to 1996.

Have conditions in the Dominican Republic improved in recent years?

The country is no longer a dictatorship. Presidents voted out of office have stepped down peacefully since 1978. But most of the country's people are desperately poor. Government officials are often corrupt. Everything from low sugar prices to hurricanes can create great hardship. Thirty percent of the people have no work. Under these conditions, Dominicans have been eager to immigrate to the United States. The only barrier has been U.S. immigration law.

When did Dominicans start coming in large numbers to the United States?

The Dominican dictator Trujillo kept tight restrictions on emigration during his reign. With his death in 1961, emigration became a way of life. In the last two decades, about 20,000 Dominicans per year have been legally admitted to the United States. (Not by coincidence, 20,000 is the legal limit for immigration from any one country.) From 1980 to 1990 alone, the official estimate of Dominican-born people residing in the United States doubled from 169,000 to 348,000. As already noted, many more Dominicans have come here unofficially.

"If the door were opened to the United States, there would be no one left to close it."

—Dominican man on the eagerness of people in his country to immigrate to the United States, early 1980s

How do undocumented immigrants from the Dominican Republic get to the United States?

There are a number of ways. Some come on a tourist visa, which allows them to visit for a short time. They overstay the visa once they're here. Some travel first to Mexico, then slip across the border into the United States.

However, the preferred route for most undocumented Dominican immigrants is to sail across the narrow Mona Passage that separates their country from Puerto Rico. The eighty-mile-wide channel is turbulent and shark-infested. Dominicans often die when their boats capsize. They may also get stopped and sent home by the border patrol. But if the emigrants make it, they can easily pretend to be Puerto Ricans, whom they resemble physically, at least to the Anglo eye. Since Puerto Rico is a U.S. territory, no passport is required to fly from there to the mainland.

Where do most Dominican immigrants settle?

The same place most Puerto Ricans settle: New York City. Since the mid-1960s, nearly three-quarters of all Dominican immigrants to the United States have settled in the Big Apple. No community besides Santo Domingo has more Dominicans.

Between 1965 and 1980, Dominicans were the largest group of immigrants to New York City. Over half of the city's Dominicans live in a single area: Washington Heights and Inwood. Others live in Corona, Queens; Manhattan's Upper West and Lower East Sides; Brooklyn's Sunset Park; and several Bronx neighborhoods.

How the Garcia Girls Lost Their Accents, a much-acclaimed 1991 novel by Dominican American Julia Alvarez, tells the story of four daughters in a Dominican immigrant family adjusting to life in the United States.

Who used to live in Washington Heights and Inwood?

These northern Manhattan neighborhoods were home to Irish and Jewish families before the 1950s. Puerto Ricans and Cubans came next, and now Dominicans—particularly on the east side of Broadway. Under the shadow of the George Washington Bridge, these neighborhoods are lively with **merengue** music and the sounds of Spanish conversation. Dominican food, similar to that of Puerto Rico and Cuba, can be found in bodegas and restaurants.

Step into the Phone Parlor

Phone parlors, or discount calling centers, are stores where immigrants can buy time to call their native countries at discounted rates. Dominicans started them for people from their own country, but now they are used by other Latinos, such as Mexicans and Peruvians. They can be found in New Jersey and in New York City—particularly in the neighborhoods of Jackson Heights and Washington Heights.

What is merengue?

This is a characteristically Dominican form of music and dance. Emerging in the nineteenth century, it combines African and Spanish influences in a fast-paced, joyous brew. Merengue bands usually include an accordion, a barrel drum called a **tambora**, and a **güiro**, or scraper. Merengue has become a popular form of dance music among Latinos in many countries.

Merengue lyrics are usually light and humorous, befitting the name—which comes from the French méringue, *the sweet, airy topping on a lemon meringue pie.*

Do Dominican immigrants usually come from the countryside?

No. There are many farm workers in the Dominican Republic, often poor and illiterate. But Dominicans who make the daring journey to the United States are usually urban people with some education and skills. When they get to the United States, they take the jobs available for people with little English: garment worker, factory hand, dishwasher. Those without legal status may accept difficult, low-paying sweatshop labor to avoid detection. Dominican

Dominican-born Oscar de la Renta became a world-renowned fashion designer. His brand name appears on clothing ranging from expensive, one-of-a-kind gowns to stylish everyday suits and dresses, as well as perfume and luggage.

Worn Anything Dominican Lately?

Fashion designer Oscar de la Renta was born in Santo Domingo, the Dominican Republic, in 1932. He studied in Madrid and opened his own salon in New York City in 1965. His luxurious, European-styled evening gowns and daywear have made him one of the most famous Dominican Americans.

Americans often live in poor neighborhoods, where lack of hope and opportunity convinces some residents to turn to street crime and drugs. But most Dominican Americans are hardworking people eager to take English-language classes, start businesses, and get ahead.

Why do so many great baseball players come from the Dominican town of San Pedro de Macorís?

No one is sure. Dozens of major league players have come from the Dominican Republic in the last twenty-five years, and many have come from this one town. Tony Fernandez of the Cleveland Indians is from there. So are Rafael Santana, Alfredo Griffin, Julio Franco, and Rico Carty.

The baseball tradition in San Pedro began early this century, when American sugar-mill owners in the town sponsored games for their employees. The Dominican taste for baseball increased during the U.S. military occupation from 1916 to 1924. Other Dominican baseball greats have included Hall-of-Fame pitcher Juan Marichal, Joaquín Andújar, and George Bell.

Pitcher Ramón Martínez plays for the Los Angeles Dodgers. He is one of the many outstanding Dominican-born players in major league baseball.

How many people of Central American origin live in the United States? ◆ What country in Central America sends the most immigrants? ◆ Which is bigger: Central America or Texas? ◆ If Central America is so small, why does it have so many countries? ◆ How big was Guatemala in Spanish colonial times? ◆ How did colonial Guatemala break up? ◆ Why isn't Panama still part of Colombia? ◆ How many Central Americans came to the United States before 1950? ◆ Why has immigration from Central America gone up since 1950? ◆ What was the original banana republic? ◆ Has the United States invested in many Central American

COMING FROM CENTRAL AMERICA

How many people of Central American origin live in the United States?

The official estimate for immigration from Central America to the United States from 1820 to 1995 is 1.1 million. Ninety percent have come just since 1960. However, this figure does not take into account the many Central Americans who have come to the United States without obtaining legal status. Fleeing civil wars, political terror, and dire poverty, they came as a matter of survival, with or without official blessing. These refugees could push the real number up by hundreds of thousands.

What country in Central America sends the most immigrants?

It is El Salvador. As of 1990, the U.S. Census Bureau estimated that 465,000 Salvadoran immigrants were living in the United States. Almost all had come in the 1980s, during the civil war that wracked their country.

The next largest group of Central American immigrants hails from Guatemala. By 1990, 226,000 were estimated to have fled the civil war in that nation. Nicaragua and Honduras have also sent large numbers of immigrants. The remaining nations of Central America—Panama, Costa Rica, and Belize—have sent fewer people.

Middle America

The seven nations that make up Central America connect the continents of North and South America

With about 33 million people, Central America is comparable in population to the state of California.

Which is bigger: Central America or Texas?

The state of Texas is bigger than the entire region of Central America. Texas has an area of about 262,000 square miles. The mountainous, heavily forested strip of land that links Mexico in North America and Colombia in South America has an area of only about 202,000 square miles. Yet it comprises seven nations: Guatemala, Belize, El Salvador, Honduras, Nicaragua, Costa Rica, and Panama.

If Central America is so small, why does it have so many countries?

The answer lies partly in how the region was carved up by imperial powers. Since colonial days, the region that is now Belize has been British rather than Spanish in culture (see the chapter Spanish America). Panama was part of Spain's colony of New Granada, and became part of Colombia when that country began to emerge from New Granada in 1819. These differences were enough to prevent Belize and Panama from uniting with the rest of Central America, which was known in colonial times simply as Guatemala, and was governed by the viceroy of New Spain.

How big was Guatemala in Spanish colonial times?

The colonial district of Guatemala stretched from present-day Mexico's southernmost state, Chiapas, through what is now Costa Rica. It included all of what are now Guatemala, El Salvador, Nicaragua, Honduras, and Costa Rica. Its capital was Antigua, which is now Guatemala City in the modern nation of Guatemala.

How did colonial Guatemala break up?

Guatemala remained part of Mexico when that country won independence from Spain (1821). Shortly afterward, in 1823, it broke away from Mexico as the United Provinces of Central America, or Central American Federation. Political conflict doomed the union. Liberals who wanted a strong federation with progressive reforms were stymied by rich conservatives who wanted to protect their wealth. Each province feared that some other province would become too powerful. By 1842, the federation had crumbled. The separate nations of Guatemala, El Salvador, Nicaragua, Honduras, and Costa Rica emerged.

Theodore Roosevelt, shown here at the age of thirty in this 1898 photograph, was strongly interested in Central and Latin America. At the time this picture was taken, he was a lieutenant colonel serving in Cuba during the Spanish American War. After he became president in 1901, he supported the Panamanian revolution of 1903 and the building of the Panama Canal.

A 1977 treaty requires the United States to turn the Panama Canal over to Panama on New Year's Day, 2000.

Why isn't Panama still part of Colombia?

In 1903, Panama revolted against Colombia and became an independent nation. Behind the revolt was American president Theodore Roosevelt. Roosevelt's policy of intervening freely in Latin American affairs has already been evident in the history of Puerto Rico, Cuba, and the Dominican Republic (see previous chapters). Following his own advice to "speak softly and carry a big stick," he carried one of his biggest sticks in Panama.

Roosevelt wanted to build a canal through Panama, one that would supply a short sea route from the Atlantic to the Pacific Oceans. The president felt such a canal was important for American economic growth and military strength. At the time, Colombia owned the territory in question, but was unwilling to cooperate with Roosevelt's plans. Roosevelt's solution: a rebellion in Panama, led by the canal's chief engineer. With the support of U.S. military forces, an independent Panama was born. The new nation gave the United States rights in perpetuity over the canal and a canal zone on either side. The canal was completed in 1914.

Building the Panama Canal was a tremendous engineering achievement. This 1909 photograph captures workers laboring in the Culebra Cut, part of the excavation for the canal.

How many Central Americans came to the United States before 1950?

Only about 71,000 came before 1950. This was a very small number compared to the millions of European immigrants who came during that time. Then the numbers started increasing. In the 1950s, 45,000 came. In the 1960s, 101,000 came. The numbers have been going up ever since. In 1995 alone, the U.S. Immigration and Naturalization Service counted 31,814 immigrants from Central America.

Why has immigration from Central America gone up since 1950?

There are several reasons, all related to Central America's civil and economic disorder. People from Panama and Honduras were mostly responsible for the first wave of Central American immigration in the 1950s and 1960s. These were mostly skilled, middle-class people seeking a better living than they could make at home.

In the 1970s, a second and bigger wave of immigrants came. These were mostly poor refugees from civil unrest and severe unemployment in El Salvador and Guatemala. A series of earthquakes and hurricanes made matters worse. In the 1980s came the biggest wave of all: hundreds of thousands of people fleeing civil war in El Salvador, Guatemala, and Nicaragua.

What was the original banana republic?

Now the name of a fashionable chain of clothing stores, "banana republic" used to be a disparaging term for any small, poor Latin American nation with a history of civil turmoil and dictatorial rule. The first country to be saddled with the insulting name may have been Honduras early this century, when American fruit companies were buying up Honduran land and using it to grow bananas. To this day, bananas are Honduras's principal crop.

Has the United States invested in many Central American countries?

Yes. Beginning in the 1840s, American companies invested millions of dollars to open mines and grow cash crops throughout Central America—especially bananas

"There appears to be nothing between these high-priced cars and the oxcart with its barefoot attendant. There is practically no middle class. ...Thirty or forty families own nearly everything in the country. They live in almost regal style. The rest of the population has practically nothing."

—American army officer visiting San Salvador, El Salvador's capital city, in the 1930s

U.S. Marines occupied Nicaragua during a period of civil turmoil from 1912 to 1933, until a stable political situation arose that served U.S. interests.

and coffee. More recently, American companies have been opening numerous factories there as well. Profits from these businesses have gone mostly into the pockets of American investors and a few wealthy Central American families.

Historically, Central American workers have been paid low wages. Land for subsistence farming has been scarce. The poor have been subject at any time to unemployment and starvation. When the poor think there is no peaceful way to improve their lot, one thing they may do is rebel—causing civil war. Another is to move away or emigrate—often to the United States.

To protect U.S. investments in Central America, the United States has often intervened with military force. In Guatemala in 1954, the United States covertly assisted in overthrowing the government of Jacobo Arbenz Guzmán. The United States disapproved of Arbenz's leftist politics. The United Fruit Company, a U.S. corporation, disliked his policy of redistributing their land to the poor.

In several countries, the United States supported **strongmen** as rulers, to keep the peace and allow American business to prosper.

What is a strongman?

A strongman or **caudillo** ("chief") is a dictator, usually the head of the army, who comes to power by military force, outlaws dissent, and jails or kills opponents. Central America has had many strongmen. Some of them have been supported by the United States with arms, military training, and financial aid.

In Nicaragua, the strongman was Anastasio Somoza (1896–1956), who ran the country, with U.S. help, from 1936 until his death. He was succeeded by his son Luis Somoza Debayle (1922–1967), who was in turn succeeded by Luis's brother Anastasio Somoza Debayle (1925–1980). In Panama, the strongman was Omar Torrijos Herrera (1929–1981), who ruled from 1968. Manuel Noriega (1934–) became the strongman after his death.

In El Salvador and Guatemala things were different. The army was almost always in charge, but the general at the head of the army often changed, as officers struggled for power. Sometimes a **junta** prevailed: a small group of military officers ruling jointly. The military served the interests of the wealthiest families and of U.S. investors. The poor remained disenfranchised, without political power.

When was the most recent civil war in El Salvador?

Civil disturbances between left-wing rebels and right-wing progovernment forces grew in the late 1970s. The conflict erupted into full-scale civil war in 1980. The spark was the murder that year of Archbishop Oscar Romero, a critic of the Salvadoran government.

The leading rebel group was the Martí National Liberation Front (FMLN). The United States accused the rebels of being communists aided by the Soviet Union and Cuba. The United States poured arms, military advisers, and economic aid into El Salvador to try to defeat the rebels. Human-rights groups gathered evidence that government forces were kidnapping, torturing, and murdering civilians suspected of aiding the rebels. The abuses were often carried out by anonymous **death squads** allied to the government.

More than 75,000 people were killed in the war. Finally, in 1992, a peace treaty ended the conflict. There was no clear victory: the rebels had not been able to overthrow the government, and the government had not been able to crush the rebels. The rebels achieved some of their goals, including a more democratic government, the creation of a new police force, and an agreement to carry out land reform to help peasants. But economic conditions in El Salvador are still bad and crime is rampant. Some of the criminals are former death squad members.

When was the civil war in Guatemala?

This conflict went on intermittently for thirty-six years, from 1960 to 1996—the longest civil war in Latin American history. Leftist guerrillas fought Guatemala's ruling elite through several presidencies and two coups (in 1963 and 1982). The government was aided heavily by the United States, which considered the guerrillas communists.

As in El Salvador, government forces and paramilitary death squads ruled through terror: kidnapping opponents,

Some of the worst violence in the Guatemalan civil war came after the 1982 coup. Suspecting that peasants were harboring the rebels, the government destroyed more than four hundred Native American villages.

torturing them, killing them. About 100,000 people were killed; another 40,000 disappeared, never to be heard from again. A million people were left homeless or driven into exile in other Central American countries, Mexico, or the United States.

A system of democratic elections was finally restored. In 1996, the rebels and the government signed a peace accord, with some concessions on each side. Whether the accord will bring lasting peace is still unknown.

Was there a civil war in Nicaragua?

There were two. The first one, in 1978–1979, overthrew the government of Anastasio Somoza Debayle. This revolution was led by the Sandinista National Liberation Front (FSLN), a left-wing group named for Augusto Cesar Sandino (1895–1934), who had waged a guerrilla war against U.S. occupation in the 1920s and '30s. The Sandinistas installed a leftist government that redistributed land to the poor, nationalized economic institutions, and improved social services. The United States called it communist. The United States accused the new Nicaragua of being a puppet for Cuba and the Soviet Union.

To try to overthrow the Sandinistas, the United States organized, funded, and trained a right-wing counterrevolutionary force called the **contras** ("against"). Based in Honduras, the contras began waging a guerrilla war in

Sandinistas guard workers harvesting coffee beans in Nicaragua. Between 1983 and 1990, the countryside was wracked by violence during the guerrilla war between the Sandinistas and U.S.-funded contras.

Nicaragua in 1983. A truce was called in 1988. In 1990, under pressure from the contras and a U.S. trade embargo, the Sandinistas held national elections and lost. Violeta Barrios de Chamorro became president. The country has been democratically ruled since then, but there is always the danger of a reversion to civil war.

What was the Iran-Contra scandal?

In 1984, Congress outlawed U.S. aid to the contras fighting the Sandinistas in Nicaragua. Officials in President Ronald Reagan's administration—notably marine lieutenant colonel Oliver North—had an idea on how to get around the ban. They illegally sold arms to Iran, then illegally used the proceeds to support the contras. The Iran-Contra scandal became public in 1986, resulting in hearings, criminal investigations, and some convictions. The people charged in the scandal were pardoned by President George Bush in 1992.

Why are people coming from Honduras and Panama? And why aren't as many coming from Costa Rica?

Honduras had its own political turmoil in the past twenty years. There were many pressures on civil order: military coups, followed by restoration of a shaky democratic government; the unpopular presence of the Nicaraguan contras; declaration of a state of emergency; a bad economy; labor strikes. Costa Rica's situation was better. It has one of Latin America's longest democratic traditions, with relatively high living standards. It long ago abolished (eliminated) its army, preventing the danger of coups.

As for Panama, it suffered a devastating invasion in 1989. The invader was the United States.

Why did the United States invade Panama?

The goal of the invasion of December 1989 was to capture dictator Manuel Noriega and force him to stand trial in the United States for drug trafficking. Noriega had been a U.S. ally during the Central American civil wars of the 1980s, but was suspected of being a middleman in bringing illegal drugs from Latin America to the United States.

Actress Madeleine Stowe is half British American, half Costa Rican. The dark-haired star of such films as The Last of the Mohicans *(1992) was born in Los Angeles in 1958.*

About 24,000 U.S. troops invaded this nation of 2.7 million people, which is a population roughly as big as Chicago's. Hundreds of Panamanians were killed. Damage was estimated at $2 billion. Democratic government was restored, but the drug trade continued and a former associate of Noriega, Ernesto Pérez Balladeres, was eventually elected president in 1994. Meanwhile, the economy was in a shambles, prompting some Panamanians to leave.

Why has it been hard for recent Central American immigrants to obtain legal status?

If newcomers to the United States can prove they are in danger of being killed or imprisoned at home for political reasons, the U.S. Immigration and Naturalization Service (INS) will allow them to stay as political refugees. But proving this case is hard, especially for people with little education and little knowledge of English. If immigrants cannot prove they are seeking political asylum, the INS assumes they came for economic reasons—to try to make money. Immigration law severely restricts how many people can immigrate for those reasons.

In the case of Central America, the problem was made worse by foreign policy issues. Nicaraguan refugees had a relatively easy time applying for political asylum when the Sandinistas were in power. The United States viewed the Sandinistas as a communist government, and therefore assumed that Nicaraguan refugees had reason to run away from them. (Even so, the refugees were at the mercy of shifting factions in the federal government, some sympathetic to them, some not.) But during the civil wars in El Salvador and Guatemala, the United States did not officially view those countries' governments to be repressive or dangerous. It didn't matter how many refugees and human rights observers testified to atrocities. How could allies of the United States be villains?

How have things changed now that the civil wars in Central America are over?

Political asylum applications are even harder to push through now that the wars have officially ended. In the United States, there remain about 300,000 refugees who applied for political asylum during the wars, and whose cases are still unresolved. Under pre-1996 law, they can stay if they can prove that they have been in the United States a certain number of years and that leaving would be an extreme hardship. New laws in 1996 placed heavier restrictions on that option, but champions of Central Americans want to give them special consideration. After all, their problems arose while their countries were at war over issues that affected the United States.

The irony is that many Central Americans left their homelands with great reluctance. They intended to go back home as soon as the danger had passed. But after a few years, they put down roots in the United States and started families. Going back is not as easy as they thought.

Central American governments have urged the United States to allow refugees to stay. Their fragile economies, shaken by years of war, could hardly stand to absorb a flood of returning exiles. Also, the region's economies depend on money that Central Americans earn in the United States and send back to families at home.

What is the sanctuary movement?

This movement is a network of churches that has guided hundreds of Central American refugees into the United States and sheltered them. In doing so, church members have risked fines and imprisonment for smuggling in undocumented aliens. They believe they have a moral obligation to protect the refugees from deportation back to their countries. Founded by Quaker Jim Corbett, the sanctuary network of churches has included all

"[B]ecause of fighting the good fight, because of being allies, because of unrest back home—there seems to be agreement... that the Central Americans... deserve special consideration."

Rep. Lamar Smith of Texas, Republican, on proposed changes in the immigration law, 1997

Driving to America

Central Americans seeking to come to the United States can drive there via the Inter-American Highway, which runs from Panama to the Mexico-Texas border. It is one part of the almost completed Pan-American Highway, a system of roads running 16,000 miles from Alaska to Chile. Those who make it as far as the U.S. border but lack documentation usually try to slip across without being caught. Others come to the United States with tourist visas, then stay after the visas expire.

denominations, and has been praised for its courage by Pope John Paul II.

Where do most Central Americans in the United States live?

Los Angeles is the home to most Central American immigrants. As of 1990, about 350,000 Salvadorans and 110,000 Guatemalans lived there. The biggest concentration of Central Americans is in the Pico-Union section west of downtown. Other favorite spots for Central Americans are San Francisco, New York, Houston, and Washington, D.C. Many Nicaraguans live in Miami.

What race are Central Americans?

It varies. Most Central Americans are a mix of European and Native American, or of African and Native American. But some are pure descendants of Native American groups such as the Maya. Mayans represent 55 percent of Guatemala's population.

What is a Ladino?

In Central America, the term means a mestizo, or person of mixed European and Native American origin. It can also mean a Native American who has chosen to adopt Spanish language and culture. The word **Ladino** also means something completely different: the language spoken by Sephardic Jews, the Jews who originated in Spain and Portugal. It includes elements of Hebrew and is sometimes called Judeo-Spanish.

What religion do Central Americans follow?

Protestants represent 30 percent of the population of Guatemala.

Most are Roman Catholic, but there are a fair number of Protestants, particularly Baptists and Evangelicals. Some Native Americans practice ancestral religions. In Guatemala, Mayan traditions have mingled with Catholic ones, producing original results—for example, the Christmas mask dance, with its colorful masks and costumes.

What is a marimba?

A **marimba** is a large wooden percussion instrument, like a xylophone. It is the national instrument of Guatemala and is played throughout Central America.

Central American music combines Spanish, Native American, and African influences. It has affinities to both Mexican and Caribbean music—rightly so, since Central America borders both regions. Some musical forms cross borders. The **nueva canción**, or "new song," movement appeared in both Nicaragua and Costa Rica. These songs denounced North American imperialism and called for social justice. But each country has its own distinctive forms. El Salvador, for example, has the **danza**, a popular dance that combines the English country dance and the Spanish **contradanza.**

What is Ruben Blades's national origin?

The singer, songwriter, and actor was born in Panama in 1948. He is committed to singing on social and political issues. His commitment was formed when American soldiers fired into a crowd of demonstrators in the Canal Zone in 1963, killing several Panamanians. Living in New York since 1974, he became a best-selling salsa artist with crossover appeal to Anglos.

What kind of work do Central Americans do in the United States?

Many do manual labor—as factory hands, farm workers, construction workers, gardeners, domestics, nannies, restaurant employees. But a number of middle-class, professional people of Central American descent also reside in the United States. They may be everything from a doctor or lawyer to a Disney animator (in the case of Jose Zeliya, who emigrated from El Salvador in 1988). Nicaraguans who fled the Sandinista revolution in 1979 were a particularly affluent group. They settled in Miami, where they had much in common with Cuban exiles who had fled Castro's revolution.

What was the movie *El Norte* about?

This 1983 film tells the story of a Guatemalan brother and sister—Native American peasants—who escape political terror in their home village to come north *(norte)* to the United States. Praised for its compassion and beauty, the film opened many people's eyes to the plight of Central American refugees.

Cello, Anyone?

Tennis player Rosemary Casals is related to famous cellist Pablo Casals—but don't remind her of that. Born in San Francisco in 1948 to parents who had immigrated from El Salvador, she is the grandniece of Pablo Casals (1876–1973). Pablo was born in Spain, moved to Puerto Rico, and is considered the greatest twentieth-century master of the cello. Rosemary won many tournaments, including five Wimbledon doubles titles with partner Billie Jean King.

She hates to be reminded of the family connection to Pablo, lest people think she somehow used it to her advantage. "I've never met the man," she once said. "If people know me, I want it to be because of what I've done."

Other great Latino tennis players have included Gabriela Sabatini, Gigi Fernandez, and Pancho Gonzalez. Arthur Ashe, known as a black tennis player, was partially of Mexican ancestry.

Multitalented Ruben Blades, right, appeared in the 1987 movie *The Milagro Beanfield War*. Blades has acted in numerous movies, including the 1985 hit *Cross-over Dreams* and director Spike Lee's 1990 release *Mo' Better Blues*. Blades is also a best-selling recording artist who won a Grammy Award for his album *Enseños*, and ran for Panamian president in 1994.

Iow many countries are there in South America?
Which has more people: South America or the United
states? ◆ How many South Americans have immigrated
o the United States? ◆ Why aren't people more aware
of South America in the United States? ◆ What
south American country sends the most immigrants
◆ Why did South Americans start coming to the United
states in larger numbers after 1950? ◆ What kind of
olitical trouble did South America have? ◆ Has the
olitical situation changed recently in South America
◆ Are most South American immigrants poor and
uneducated? ◆ Why don't South Americans who wa

COMING FROM SOUTH AMERICA

How many countries are there in South America?

The continent of South America is divided into thirteen distinct political entities. One, French Guiana, is an overseas department, or province, of France. The other twelve are independent nations. Of these, nine are Hispanic: Argentina, Bolivia, Chile, Colombia, Ecuador, Paraguay, Peru, Uruguay, and Venezuela. Three are non-Hispanic: Guyana, Suriname, and Brazil (see the chapter Spanish America for explanations of their history).

Which has more people: South America or the United States?

South America does, by about 20 percent. As of 1995, there were 319.6 million South Americans compared to 265.1 million people in the United States. Spanning 6.9 million square miles, South America is about twice as big in land area as the United States. Most of its people are clustered along its edges; much of the interior is sparsely populated. The terrain of South America includes everything from the snowcapped peaks of the Andes Mountains to the tropical jungles of the Amazon River Valley, from the bone-dry Atacama Desert of Chile to the **pampas,** or prairies, of Argentina.

Who's Biggest?

In terms of population, all of South America's Hispanic countries are dwarfed by Brazil, with its 163 million people. In fact, most of the countries in this list have fewer people than California, with its 32 million residents. In descending order of population, the countries are:

Colombia: 37 million
Argentina: 35 million
Peru: 25 million
Venezuela: 22 million
Chile: 14 million
Ecuador: 11 million
Bolivia: 7 million
Paraguay: 6 million
Uruguay: 3 million

In terms of land area, the biggest Hispanic country in South America is Argentina, with 1.1 million square miles—about a third of Brazil's and a little less than a third of the United States's. The smallest is Uruguay: at 68,000 square miles, it is about the size of Oklahoma.

How many South Americans have immigrated to the United States?

According to the Immigration and Naturalization Service, 1.5 million South Americans have come to the United States from 1820 to 1995. Most of them have come from South America's Hispanic nations. Ninety-one percent have come just since 1950, and 85 percent since 1960. In the 1980s alone, 456,000 South Americans were admitted to the United States. The actual numbers may be greater, since an unknown number of additional South Americans have come here illegally.

These figures show that people of South American descent are a substantial and growing percentage of the nation's Hispanic Americans. Their current numbers are comparable to the number of people of Cuban or Dominican descent. However, many people in the United States are barely aware of South Americans as a distinct group.

Why aren't people more aware of South Americans in the United States?

Perhaps because South American immigrants tend not to think of themselves as South American, or even as Hispanic. They identify with their home country—Ecuador or Peru, for example. In many cases, these countries have long been rivals or enemies. An Ecuadoran might be insulted to be mistaken for a Peruvian—something like an English-man being mistaken for a Frenchman during the Napoleonic Wars.

Because no single South American country has had a large community in the United States for a prolonged period, most Americans are unaware that there are any Americans of South American descent. There are—and their numbers are increasing.

What South American country sends the most immigrants?

As of 1990, it was Colombia. In that year, the U.S. Census Bureau counted 286,000 Colombian-born Americans. Most were recent immigrants: their numbers nearly doubled since 1980, when the total was 144,000.

Ecuador and Peru also send large numbers of immigrants. Like Colombia, these countries occupy the north-

The continent of South America encompasses both the Andes Mountains, which run like a backbone down its length, and the giant Amazon River basin. Home to the world's largest tropical rain forest and rich in minerals, South America has been troubled by political and economic unrest throughout its history and much of its population remains poor.

west part of South America, and are therefore closer to the United States than most other South American countries. But immigrants come from every nation in South America—Venezuela, Argentina, Chile, and elsewhere.

Why did South Americans start coming to the United States in larger numbers after 1950?

Three words: commercial air travel. By the end of World War II, commercial flights to the United States had come within the reach of middle-class South Americans. If they could afford a plane ticket, they could come.

They had reason to come because of both economic and political turmoil in their home countries. The continent's population more than doubled between 1960 and 1990, straining resources. (The U.S. population went up only 39 percent in the same period.) After World War II, many nations launched programs to modernize and industrialize their economies. To some extent, the programs succeeded: financed by foreign banks, many South American economies grew at a brisk pace until the 1980s. Petroleum exporting, particularly in Venezuela, became a big business.

But the gap between rich and poor, always great in South America, did not significantly shrink. And with industrialization came new problems. As agriculture became mechanized, many farmers were thrown out of work. Others sought to escape the age-old hardships of Latin American peasant existence for what they thought would be a better life in the booming cities of the continent. The result was overcrowded urban areas with many unemployed or barely employed people. Destitute families lived in wretched shantytowns surrounding glittering cities.

What kind of political trouble did South America have?

Political instability has plagued the continent throughout its history. Ever since achieving independence, the nations of South America have been famous for their frequent revolutions and coups. Constitutions and elected presidents give way to dictators and juntas and new constitutions and presidents. The 1960s and 1970s were a particularly stormy time. The military took power in Ecuador

Gauchos relax on the *pampas* of South America. These cattle herders follow a way of life hundreds of years old. However, as South America's economies modernize, ranching and agriculture have changed dramatically, and many rural dwellers are forced to move to urban areas and, often, to emigrate.

in 1972, Uruguay in 1973, Argentina in 1976, and in Peru in 1962, 1968, and 1975. Leftist guerrillas fought the government of Bolivia in the 1960s and of Colombia in the 1970s. In Chile in 1973, the elected government of left-wing president Salvador Allende was overthrown, reportedly with covert U.S. help, by right-wing dictator Augusto Pinochet. In Chile and Argentina, right-wing governments ruled by terror, killing and kidnapping anyone even suspected of dissent.

Has the political situation gotten any better in South America?

Yes. During the 1980s and 1990s, the military dictatorships and juntas fell by the wayside. For the moment, democratically elected governments prevail across the continent. But in every country there is always the danger of a return to military rule.

Problems continue. In the 1980s and '90s, both Peru and Colombia fought wars against guerrilla armies. In the 1980s, an international recession afflicted many South American economies. Prices climbed and many people

In what was called the Dirty War, a military junta that took power in Argentina in 1976 fought its suspected opponents by kidnapping and murdering them. More than nine thousand people are believed to have disappeared in this way.

In December 1996, left-wing rebels belonging to the Tupac Amaru movement took over the Japanese ambassador's residence in Lima, Peru, seizing over seventy hostages. Four months later, President Alberto Fujimori ended the stand-off with a commando raid that rescued the hostages and killed all the rebels.

were unable to find work. South American governments had long depended on large loans from foreign banks, but now they were unable to pay back the loans or even, in some cases, make interest payments.

Governments tried several measures to try to improve their economies. One tactic was to cut spending on social services. This was painful to many people, especially the poor who depended on government relief. Governments also tried changing state-owned businesses into privately owned ones, hoping these would be more successful at making money. In many cases, the private companies started their existence by firing people.

Faced with such economic and political turbulence, it is no wonder that many South Americans have sought refuge in the United States over the last few decades. Some of these immigrants plan to return home when conditions improve. Some do return home after a few years. But many others put down roots and stay.

Are most South American immigrants poor and uneducated?

On the whole, South American immigrants to the United States tend to be better educated and more prosperous than other Hispanic newcomers. They tend to be middle-class people with technical skills and a strong belief in education. Many come from cities rather than rural areas.

One reason: travel to the United States is expensive. It is hard for a poor person to afford the airfare. The distance to New York City from Lima, Peru, is greater than that from London, England. Another is that middle-class people have the most to lose from such problems as high inflation and governments that penalize a person for belonging to the wrong party.

With their education and skills, South Americans tend to adapt readily to life in the United States. Because of a lack of English or necessary credentials, they may be forced at first to accept lower-status jobs than they might have held in their native country: a lawyer working as a clerk; an engineer working in a factory. But many eventually achieve a standard of living higher than what they could have had at home.

Why don't South Americans who want to emigrate go to other South American countries instead of the United States?

They do. Many South Americans seeking a better life go to other countries on the continent. Colombians, for example, often move to neighboring Venezuela, Ecuador, or Panama. Peruvians may emigrate to Chile, Paraguay, or Argentina. Some feel they will have an easier time in a foreign country that shares their language and some common elements of Latino culture. On the other hand, during periods when all of Latin America is suffering similar economic woes, the best choice is to go outside the region to some place that isn't—like the United States.

Do South Americans ever travel illegally to the United States?

Yes. They use the same methods as other undocumented immigrants from Latin America. Some first travel to Mexico and are smuggled into the United States over the border. Others visit the United States on tourist visas, then quietly stay after the visas expire.

Where is the largest community of South Americans in the United States?

It is in Jackson Heights, a neighborhood in the borough of Queens in New York City. South Americans first started coming there at the end of World War I. Many Colombians now live there; some call it "Chapinero," after a suburb of Bogotá. The neighborhood is also home to Latinos from other parts of the Americas. The business district is stocked with Latino restaurants, newsstands, travel and real estate agencies, and grocery stores. The Italian, Irish, and Jewish immigrants who once lived in Jackson Heights have mostly moved elsewhere.

Substantial numbers of South Americans can also be found in Florida and California. But they live everywhere, from Boston to Chicago to Oregon. Viewing themselves as distinct from more typical Hispanic American groups, such as Mexicans and Puerto Ricans, they may choose to live among Anglos rather than in a Hispanic American barrio. Often, their children readily assimilate into Anglo society.

In the heavily Hispanic section of New York City called Jackson Heights, you can buy Colombian magazines and Colombian newspapers from Bogotá and fifteen different provinces.

In 1994, Carlos Manzano was elected a Democratic state committeeman— becoming the first Colombian-born elected official in New York City history.

What is the racial makeup of South America's Hispanics?

It varies greatly. Many are mestizos (a mix of European and Native American), but there are also mulattoes, blacks, pure whites, and pure Native Americans. In the highlands of Andean nations live many Native Americans, representing 45 percent of Peru's population and 55 percent of Bolivia's. In Argentina and Uruguay, there are virtually no Native Americans and few mestizos: 85 percent of Argentina's people and 90 percent of Uruguay's are of pure European descent. People of African descent live in coastal areas of such nations as Venezuela, Colombia, and Ecuador.

What are costeños?

Costeños are people from northern coastal Colombia who are of mixed African, Spanish, and Native American descent. At home, they live in cities such as Cartagena. In the United States, many live in New York and Chicago. Both in the United States and Colombia, *costeños* tend to keep apart from pure white Colombians, who have historically received social and economic privileges. Whites, blacks, and mulattoes are all minorities in Colombia, where 58 percent of the population is mestizo.

Are all Colombians drug dealers?

No, but this stereotype haunts Colombians. Colombia is the world's foremost exporter of cocaine. Colombian drug cartels (associations), notably those in Medellín and Cali, have associates and hirelings in many countries, including the United States. The United States has accused Colombian president Ernesto Samper, elected in 1994, of soliciting and accepting contributions from the drug traffickers. But despite all the high-profile news reports, most Colombian immigrants are law-abiding people, not drug dealers.

Did any South American country ever have a president born in the United States?

Yes. The first South American president to be born in the United States was Galo Plaza Lasso, president of Ecuador from 1948 to 1952. The son of Ecuador's minister to the United States, he was born in New York City's Greenwich Village in 1906. Ecuador seems to like American-born presidents: Sixto Durán Ballén, born in Boston in 1921, served as Ecuador's president from 1992 to 1996. An architect, he was educated at Columbia University and the University of Wisconsin.

Why does South America produce so many architects?

The discipline of architecture is held in high esteem in South America. One example is Cesar Pelli, who was born in Argentina in 1922 and immigrated to the United States. In the 1960s and '70s, he earned acclaim for such projects as the Vienna International Center and the World Financial Towers in Manhattan. In 1977, he became dean of the architecture school at Yale University.

What is Quechua?

Quechua is a family of Native American languages spoken in the Andes Mountains of South America. It includes the tongue spoken by the Incas in Peru before the Spanish conquistadors arrived. Quechuan languages are still spoken by Native Americans of Peru, Ecuador, Bolivia, and other South American countries. Many Quechuan words have passed into Spanish and from there into English. These include *poncho, llama, puma, condor,* and *gaucho.*

What does "El Condor Pasa" mean?

The title of the 1970 Simon and Garfunkel song means "the **condor** passes." It refers to the majestic vulture of the Andes. With its ten-foot wingspan and bald red head, the condor is regarded as a good omen by the Aymara, a Native American people of Peru and Bolivia.

Based on an eighteenth-century Peruvian folk melody, the Simon and Garfunkel song showcased Andean Native American music. This music builds on the Incan pentatonic (five-tone) scale. Plaintive and high-pitched, it is played on panpipes of cane or bone, drums, flutes, and conch shell trumpets.

Tapioca, a starch used in puddings, is a Guarani word.

Since breaking up with Art Garfunkel, American musician Paul Simon has picked up many other ideas from Latin American and African music. In the 1970s, he toured with the Peruvian ensemble Urubamba. His 1986 *Graceland* album included music by Los Lobos. His 1998 Broadway musical *The Capeman* told the story of Sal Agron, a Puerto Rican youth convicted of a double murder in New York City in 1959 who went on to become a prison poet.

Do the cumbia and tango come from the same country?

No, but both Latin dances come from South America. The **cumbia** comes from Colombia, where bands called **vallenato** ensembles play the music that goes with it. Instruments include a diatonic button accordion, drums, shakers, and scrapers. The music combines Spanish, Native American, and African influences.

The **tango** is a graceful, romantic ballroom dance that originated in Argentina and spread to international popularity in the early twentieth century. Like the cumbia, it is popular among Hispanic Americans from many countries.

What is the ethnic background of singer Mariah Carey?

The Grammy-winning pop music star was born in 1970 in New York City. Her father was a Venezuelan of African descent, her mother Irish. She is the latest in a long tradition of musicians of South American descent who made it big in the United States. Another is Bolivian violinist Jaime Laredo (born in 1941), who has toured internationally to great success since the 1950s. He has lived in the United States since coming here to study the violin at age seven in 1948.

Who are the Guarani?

They are a Native American people who once lived widely in central and southern South America. Small populations still live in Paraguay, Uruguay, Argentina, and Brazil; some still practice their traditional communal agriculture. In Paraguay, their influence has been especially strong. Ninety percent of the country's largely mestizo pop-

Kiss of the Novelist

The 1976 novel *The Kiss of the Spider Woman* is the story of two men sharing a prison cell in a politically repressive South American country. It was written by an Argentine named Manuel Puig who knew political repression firsthand: he fled his troubled country in 1973 to live in Mexico and New York City. Though based on the unhappy realities of South American life, the novel was a big success. It was turned into a movie that netted a Best Actor Oscar for its star, William Hurt, and a Broadway musical that won several top Tony awards.

ulation speak Guarani. Guarani songs, dances, poems, and myths are an important part of Paraguay's heritage.

Have any South American writers won the Nobel Prize in literature?

Yes. The first was Chilean poet Gabriela Mistral, born Lucila Godoy Alcayaga (1889–1957). She won the 1945 Nobel Prize in Literature for her passionate, lyrical poetry. Though born in Chile, she was a teacher and diplomat who spent much of her life abroad—in Mexico, Europe, and the United States—and died in New York.

Mistral was the first South American, or Latin American, writer to be honored with the Nobel Prize in literature, but not the last. Other South Americans have included Chilean poet Pablo Neruda (1971) and Colombian novelist Gabriel García Márquez (1982). Octavio Paz, a Mexican poet, was awarded the prize in 1990. He died at the age of 84 in 1998.

Besides those mentioned, great South American writers have included Ecuadoran Jorgé Icaza, author of the novel *Huasipungo* (1934), which dealt with the exploitation of Native Americans. Another is Uruguayan poet Juan Zorilla de San Martín, author of the 1886 epic poem *Tabaré*.

Do Spanish-speaking people ever come to the United States from Spain, or do they only come from Latin America? ◆ How do the numbers of Spanish immigrants compare to those from other countries in Europe? Is a Spanish American the same thing as an Iberian American? ◆ When was the largest period of Spanish immigration? Do immigrants still come to the United States through Ellis Island? ◆ Where did Spanish immigrants mostly settle? ◆ Who are the Basques? Where do most Basque Americans live? ◆ What language does the name "jai alai" come from? ◆ What was the Abraham Lincoln Battalion? ◆ What was th

COMING FROM SPAIN

Do Spanish-speaking people ever come to the United States from Spain, or do they only come from Latin America?

So many Hispanic Americans trace their roots to Latin American countries that you might think Spain long ago closed its doors to emigration. In fact, Spanish relocation to North America did not end with the conquistadors. Throughout its history, the United States has been the destination of a small but steady procession of Spanish immigrants.

How do the numbers of Spanish immigrants compare to those from other countries in Europe?

About 244,000 Spanish people crossed the Atlantic Ocean to come to the United States between 1820 and 1974. By comparison, about 25 million Germans and 9 million Italians came to the United States between 1820 and 1974. That means about one Spaniard crossed the Atlantic for every 139 Germans and Italians.

Is a Spanish American the same thing as an Iberian American?

Not quite. The Iberian Peninsula is mostly occupied by Spain, but it also includes Portugal. Iberian Americans can come from either country.

The famous Rock of Gibraltar is a limestone promontory connected to southern Spain by a sandy strip of land. Populated by about 30,000 people, it has belonged to Britain since the eighteenth century.

When was the largest period of Spanish immigration?

Between 1901 and 1931, when 100,000 Spanish immigrants came to the United States. Steamship travel, widely available in this period, made the trip faster and more comfortable than the sailing ships of the nineteenth century. Most of those who came were farmers or tradespeople tired of poverty and political turmoil at home. Some were young men trying to escape military service. For a time, Spain forbade emigration, but citizens fled anyway. Many left from Gibraltar, a British colony on the Iberian Peninsula.

Do immigrants still come to the United States through Ellis Island?

No. This immigrant receiving station near Manhattan opened in 1892 and closed in 1954. During that time, about 20 million immigrants passed through its gates, including those from Spain. Like all immigrants, those from Spain, had to pass medical tests and convince examiners they could support themselves. If they failed to do so, they were sent back to Spain.

Were Spanish immigrants welcome in the United States?

Spanish newcomers were treated with a similar level of prejudice as other immigrants from southern Europe, such as Italians. Many in America preferred immigrants who had lighter skins and came from northern climates, like England and Scandinavia. This prejudice was embodied in a quota system first enacted in 1921 and later became still

Aloha, Spanish Immigrants

Between 1906 and 1913, Hawaii was a popular destination for Spanish immigrants because work could be found there in the sugarcane fields. During those years, about eight thousand Spanish immigrants came to the South Pacific islands of Hawaii—then a U.S. possession and now a state. Most of these Spanish Americans later settled near San Francisco, California.

more restrictive. According to a 1929 version of the law, northern Europeans were welcome in large numbers— 132,000 per year. Southern and eastern Europe and Asia were permitted to send no more than 20,000 people to the United States. Spain's allotment was 131 per year.

The quota system was abolished in 1965. Currently, all countries have the same ceiling: no more than 20,000 immigration visas per country per year.

Where did Spanish immigrants mostly settle?

Better educated and skilled than many of the immigrants who came through Ellis Island in the early twentieth century, Spanish newcomers often stayed in New York City. Some traveled west to work as ranchers or farmers. Tampa, Florida, was also home to a large Spanish American community.

Who are the Basques?

Basques are a people with an unusual distinction: they are Europe's oldest known ethnic group. To look at them, you might think they are Spanish, but their homeland, known as the Basque country, straddles both southwest France and northern Spain. Their native language is not Spanish but Basque, which has no known ties to any other language. Even their blood is distinctive. They almost never have type B or AB blood, but they have the highest incidence of type O and Rh-negative factor of any ethnic group in the world.

Privately, Basques call themselves Euskaldunaks, speakers of the language Euskera. Basque was the name given to them by the ancient Romans.

Basques are believed to have lived in their homeland since the Stone Age, retaining ancient customs despite wave after wave of invaders. Some came to the New World with the conquistadors; others came to the United States directly from Spain or France.

Where do most Basque Americans live?

They settled mainly in Nevada, Idaho, and Oregon, along with some other parts of the West, including California and Wyoming. They first came to the United States in the mid-nineteenth century. Skilled as shepherds, Basque immigrants found work in that business and came to dominate the sheepherding industry of the West. Most

A Basque shepherd stands with part of his herd in north-eastern Nevada. The Basques, from northern Spain, thrived in sheep ranching in the arid West.

were poor when they came, but as they prospered, their families turned to other, less difficult occupations—such as politics. Senator Paul Laxalt of Nevada is a descendant of Basque immigrants.

What language does the name "jai alai" come from?

The unusual name of this fast-moving game comes from Basque: it means "joyous festival." Cuban Basques brought it to the United States in 1924. It is popular today in Florida and Connecticut, where betting on the game is legal. Also called pelota (Spanish for "ball"), the game is played with a hard rubber ball and wicker baskets attached to the players' arms.

What was the Abraham Lincoln Battalion?

It was a battalion of about 2,800 volunteers from the United States who traveled to Spain to fight for the Republican cause in the Spanish civil war (1936–1939). With similar volunteer units from more than fifty other countries, it was part of the International Brigades. The Abraham

Lincoln Battalion, also known as the Lincoln Brigade, saw action at the Battle of Jaroma in 1937. The International Brigades were withdrawn in 1938.

What was the fighting about in the Spanish civil war?

The war started in 1936 when General Francisco Franco (1892–1975) led a revolt against the Spanish Republic. Franco was a fascist, which meant he believed in a dictatorial, militaristic form of government. Germany and Italy, both fascist states at the time, sent arms and advisers to support Franco's group, known as the Nationalists, against the Loyalists, or Republicans. About one million people died in the civil war, which ended with Franco's victory. Many people fled Spain for the United States and other countries to escape the horrors of war and the repressive rule of Franco.

What kind of name is "Capote"?

The last name of American writer Truman Capote (1924–1984) is Spanish. Of Spanish American descent, he was born in New Orleans, Louisiana. He became well known

A **jai alai** player in action displays the long, specially shaped basket used to catch and fling the pelota, or ball. He wears a helmet because the rubber pelota can reach dangerous speeds as it rockets around the small enclosed court where *jai alai* is played.

for his novella *Breakfast at Tiffany's* (1958) and his "nonfiction novel" *In Cold Blood* (1966), an account of the real-life mass murder of a rural Kansas family. Celebrated in literary circles, the short, witty writer was known for being open about his homosexuality at a time when few people were.

Who are some other famous twentieth-century Spanish Americans?

One is the actor Martin Sheen. He was born Ramon Estevez in Ohio in 1940 to a Spanish immigrant father and Irish American mother. His most famous film is probably *Apocalypse Now* (1979). His sons Emilio Estevez and Charlie Sheen are also movie stars.

The winner of the 1968 Nobel Prize for physics was Spanish American Luis W. Alvarez (1911–1988). He won the award for his research on the detection and nature of subatomic particles. His son, Walter Alvarez, is a geologist. In 1979, the father and son together proposed the influential theory that an asteroid or comet caused the extinction of the dinosaurs.

For what did Severo Ochoa win the Nobel Prize?

Born in 1905, the Spanish-born molecular biologist fled war in Europe to come to the United States in 1941. For thirty-two years, beginning in 1942, he taught at New York University. One of his interests was RNA (ribonucleic acid), a compound found in living cells that is important in cell reproduction. Ochoa isolated an enzyme that allowed him to perform the first test-tube synthesis of RNA. His discovery helped open the way for modern genetic engineering.

Exit a Nobel Prize Winner

Among the people who fled Spain during the Spanish civil war was a future Nobel Prize winner: poet Juan Ramón Jimenez (1881–1958). He was one of many intellectuals opposed to Franco who emigrated at this time. He lived in Cuba for a while, then in the United States, where he taught at the University of Maryland. Author of such poetry collections as *Unidad* (*Unity*, 1925), he won the Nobel Prize for literature in 1956. He died two years later in Puerto Rico.

Popular movie actor Martin Sheen is of Spanish American descent. His two sons, Emilio Estevez and Charlie Sheen, have followed him into film careers.

For his research, he became corecipient of the 1959 Nobel Prize in physiology or medicine. In 1985, Ochoa returned to his native Spain, where he lived until his death in 1993.

Does Spain still have a king, like in colonial times?

Yes—but the king's power is restrained by law. The current ruler is King Juan Carlos I, who succeeded Franco upon the dictator's death in 1975. Born in 1938, Juan Carlos helped Spain make the transition from autocratic to democratic rule. As a constitutional monarchy, the country is governed by the *Cortes*, or parliament.

Spain has been without a monarch for only three periods since Christopher Columbus's day: during the first republic (1873–1874), the second republic (1931–1939), and Franco's dictatorship (1939–1975).

Man on the Verge of a Hollywood Breakthrough

Americans first started noticing Antonio Banderas in a 1988 film called *Women on the Verge of a Nervous Breakdown*. This dark comedy from Spain played to great acclaim in the United States. Its director, Pedro Almodóvar, became internationally known, as did Banderas, a star of this and other Almodóvar films. The actor has since come to Hollywood to be a leading man in such American films as *Desperado* (1995). That film was directed by Robert Rodriguez, a Hispanic American from Texas who made his name with the Spanish-language film *El Mariachi (1992)*.

How many immigrants are still coming from Spain?

Not many. In 1995, 1,321 came—far fewer than the 89,932 admitted from Mexico. Nowadays, the annual immigration from Spain is roughly equivalent to the numbers from the Netherlands or the former Czechoslovakia.

HISPANIC AMERICAN LIFE

Are Hispanic Americans one big happy family?

Not necessarily. Hispanic immigrants to the United States often think of themselves first as nationals of a particular country—Mexico, Cuba, El Salvador, the Dominican Republic, Ecuador. Their U.S.-born children or grandchildren may become so assimilated to Anglo culture that they think of themselves as Americans rather than Hispanic Americans.

There is considerable discord between Hispanic American communities. Some of it is has a racial element. White Cuban Americans in Miami may resent being lumped together with mulatto Puerto Ricans or mestizo Mexican Americans. Some of it stems from competition for the same jobs and opportunities. Puerto Ricans who have fought hard for economic and political position in New York may resent Dominicans, who they see as interlopers, or intruders. Dominicans, in turn, may see Puerto Ricans as clannish people blocking them from success.

Even so, Hispanic Americans are increasingly conscious of the need to band together on social and political issues that affect them all, such as racism and immigration policy. And they share enough features in common—the Spanish language; widespread Catholic faith; beliefs about the value of family—that they are usually glad to meet a fellow Latino, from whatever country.

John Leguizamo, who became a movie actor after writing and starring in such one-man stage shows as Mambo Mouth, *is a mix of Colombian and Puerto Rican. He continued his solo stage work with* Freak.

Do Hispanic Americans ever marry outside their national group?

Yes, often. In this, they show the willingness to mix that has always been part of Hispanic culture. The practice tends to break down walls between communities. When a Mexican American marries a Puerto Rican, the common bond between Hispanics is strengthened. When their child marries an Anglo, the bond between Hispanics and their adopted country becomes stronger.

Do Hispanics from one country get mistaken for Hispanics from another country?

All the time. As a rule, Anglos on the West Coast assume every Hispanic they meet is from Mexico. Anglos on the East Coast assume all Hispanics are from Puerto Rico (except for Miami Anglos, who think they are all from Cuba). There are exceptions: in the 1990s, an Ecuadoran immigrant in Brooklyn, New York, was beaten up by Anglo youths calling him a "Mexican." Hispanic Americans spend a lot of time simply explaining what they are not.

Are Hispanic Americans Democrats or Republicans?

During the 1988 presidential election, Republican Latino politician Gaddi Vasquez commented on Democrat Michael Dukakis, the losing candidate: "The Democratic candidate may speak Spanish, but he doesn't speak our language." Many, though not all, Hispanic Americans felt the liberal Dukakis was out of touch with their concerns.

Sixty-five percent call themselves Democrats, and most elected Latinos in Congress are Democrats. But Democratic candidates should not assume that Latinos vote strictly by party. Traditional Democratic issues—civil rights, immigrants' rights, social programs to aid the poor—are important to Latinos. But so are such Republican watchwords as law and order, family values, and support for religion and parochial schools. In fact, the Republican Party gets more money in campaign contributions from Latinos than does the Democratic Party. The reason is that the most affluent Hispanic Americans tend to be Cuban exiles, who have money to donate and are usually Republican. (See the chapter Coming from Cuba for an explanation.)

The divided loyalties of Hispanic Americans have kept them from becoming a monolithic voting bloc. It has also kept politicians from taking their votes for granted. This is important, given that the number of Hispanic American voters is growing several times faster than the electorate as a whole.

How many Hispanics are in public office?

There are more than five thousand Hispanic elected officials in the United States, including about twenty members of the U.S. House of Representatives. President Bill Clinton's first-term cabinet included two Hispanics: Henry Cisneros, secretary of housing and urban development, and Federico Peña, secretary of transportation. Of the two, only Peña stayed on in Clinton's second term, as secretary of energy.

Who was the first Hispanic mayor of a major American city?

It was Henry Cisneros (1947–), future U.S. cabinet member. He was mayor of San Antonio, Texas, the nation's ninth largest city, from 1982 to 1990.

Why don't you see the Chiquita Banana girl much anymore?

For the same reason you don't see the Frito Bandido anymore. These character trademarks were staples of TV commercials of the 1960s. They were popular with Anglo American audiences but offended many Hispanic Americans. The Fritos corn chip bandit suggested a sterotype of Mexicans as sleazy criminals. The Chiquita Banana girl made Latinos seem silly and childish. As Hispanic Americans came of age as a political force, they were increasingly vocal in objecting to such stereotypes.

What is the origin of the term "spic"?

Some scholars think this insulting name for a Latino is related to how Latinos pronounce the word "speak," as in "No spic English." However, it was applied to Italian Americans before being targeted against Hispanics, and might be an abbreviation of "spaghetti."

What is the origin of the term "gringo"?

Many possible origins have been suggested for this term, a disparaging name used by Latinos to refer to Anglos. Some people think it originated in the phrase Mexicans used to yell to green-coated U.S. troops during the Mexican War: "Green, go!" But the phrase is found all over Latin America, not just in Mexico. More likely it evolved from the Spanish word for "gibberish," **gringo**, which is related to the word for "Greek," griego. In other words, when a gringo talks, it's all Greek to some Latinos.

What stereotypes do Hispanic Americans have about Anglos?

Anglo prejudice against Hispanic Americans is matched only by Hispanic American prejudice against Anglos. Many Latinos think of Anglos as cold, materialistic, and money-grubbing. By contrast, Latinos see themselves as warm, family-oriented, community-minded people. One Colombian said of Anglos: "They don't care for their fellow man, be it their father, son, or neighbor. They only care for *el numero uno*." Latinos see themselves as humanists who appreciate world culture, but Anglos are said to appreciate nothing but Anglo-Saxon culture.

The mutual stereotyping takes place internationally as well as domestically. Historically, U.S. leaders have seen Latin American nations as corrupt, violent, childlike places that need to be corrected by the strong hand of U.S. intervention. Latin Americans have felt anger at North American paternalism (acting like a father with his children) and exploitation and the North American hunger to send in the marines. Even some conservative

Hasta la Vista, Baby

The link between machismo and Latino culture is strong. It is so strong that Anglos who would like to seem tough often try to identify themselves with Hispanic culture. Nowhere is this more true than in movies and TV. Clint Eastwood wore a poncho in his westerns. As a Secret Service agent in *In the Line of Fire* (1993), he called his gun a *pistola*. Cartoon bad-boy Bart Simpson knows enough Spanish to say, *"Ay caramba!"* whenever he is taken aback.

One of the toughest hombres ("men") of all was an android: the killer cyborg in *Terminator 2* (1991). When blowing away enemies, the Austrian-accented cyborg played by Arnold Schwarzenegger liked to say a Spanglish goodbye: *"Hasta la vista, baby."*

Latin Americans have taken satisfaction in seeing communist Fidel Castro defy the United States for so long.

What is machismo?

The Spanish word for male is **macho**. **Machismo** is the Latino idea of what it means to be a man. It includes such notions as courage, virility, honor, toughness. It usually implies that men are superior to women and rightfully hold authority over them. At its noblest, machismo means providing for one's family, keeping one's word, standing up for what is right. At its crudest, it means violence, swagger, sexual prowess, and domination of women.

Virtually all Latino males are aware of the concept, though whether or how they carry it out varies greatly. Anglos tend to know the word machismo only in the cheap, ridiculous sense embodied in the Village People song "Macho Man."

How do Latina women feel about machismo?

For Latin American women, the ideology of machismo has often meant oppression and second-class status. Many accept the authority of men as an inescapable part of life, whether it is legitimate or not. Latinas in the United States have greater freedom than in their home countries to earn a living and be respected as equals of men. Some reject the idea of machismo altogether, believing that men and women alike should strive toward the same ideal of being human.

Why do Hispanics have two last names?

In Spain and Latin America, a child is given both its father's last name and its mother's maiden name. For example, Anita Castillo Sánchez would be the daughter of a father named Castillo and a mother whose maiden name was Sánchez. The mother is thereby honored along with the father, though her name will drop out in subsequent generations. For example, if Anita has a daughter Josefina by a man named Martínez, the daughter is born Josefina Martínez Castillo; the name Sánchez disappears.

In the United States, Hispanics usually streamline their two last names down to one—the father's name.

As a sign of the Hispanic belief in family, Hispanic households in the United States are more likely than non-Hispanic ones to be made up of two parents raising minor children. The proportion is 37 percent for Hispanic households versus 25 percent for non-Hispanic ones.

Why are relatives frequent visitors to many Hispanic American households?

In the United States, the nuclear family—mother, father, children—is by far the most important unit of kinship. In Latin America, the nuclear family is one part of a vast extended family of grandparents, uncles, aunts, and cousins, who live close together and help each other out. Moving to the United States breaks up these family networks, but Hispanic Americans try to keep up the links as best they can. They send money back to the old country to support family members, sponsor relatives to come join them, and visit the old country frequently.

What is a compadre?

A **compadre** is literally a coparent. When a Latino child is born, the parents choose good friends to be *compadres*—often the godmother and godfather (**madrina** or **padrino**) at the child's baptism. The compadre is expected to be a second parent throughout the child's life, keeping in contact and helping out as needed. The system is called **compadrazgo**.

Why do so many Catholic churches in the United States now have Spanish masses?

A growing minority of Latinos are Protestant, but the vast majority remain Roman Catholic. Like many other Catholics, they do not always observe all the church's rules, but they get their kids baptized and often make financial sacrifices to send them to parochial school. The Virgin Mary and the saints are honored with pictures and statuettes. The church's fiestas, or feast days, are an important part of Hispanic American cultural life.

As the number of Hispanic Americans mushroomed since the 1950s, the Catholic church in the United States changed to keep up with them. In urban areas with large Latino populations, priests are often fluent in Spanish and churches offer weekly masses in Spanish, usually with vibrant Latino music.

About one-third of the nation's 60 million Catholics are of Hispanic origin.

What's the Hispanic American stand on bilingual education?

There is no single stand. Many agree that children who have just immigrated should be allowed to pursue some studies in Spanish until English mastery is achieved. Children who speak no English cannot reasonably be expected to just pick it up without having their grades suffer. On the other hand, some Americans—Latinos included—think bilingual education can go too far. They are opposed to creating a separate bilingual track for Hispanic Americans that dooms them to an inferior education. Other Latinos think bilingual education does not go far enough. Why not require all students to be educated in Spanish language and Latino culture?

Behind the debate on bilingual education is a deeper issue. Many Americans fear that their English-speaking culture is threatened by the growing population of Hispanic Americans. This fear is behind the recent spate of English-only laws that would make English the official language of a given town or state.

According to a 1996 poll, 51 percent of Hispanic American parents said that learning to read, write, and speak English was the most important goal of their children's education.

Do all Hispanic Americans speak Spanish the same way?

No. There are many variations in dialect. In New Mexico, a relatively pure form of sixteenth- and seventeenth-century Spanish has been preserved from the days before the region was conquered by the United States. Many Chicanos of Texas and California speak Pachuco, a slang that includes Mexican expressions and English-derived terms. The fast-paced

Spanglish Spoken Here

Spanglish is the informal name for a brand of Spanish peppered with borrowed words or phrases from English. Even in Latin America, some Hispanics routinely use words like *lonche* (for "lunch") or *jonrón* (for "home run") because the word pleases the ear or best expresses a certain shade of meaning. Puerto Ricans like to throw a **pahry**—from the English "party"—and shop at a **marqueta** ("market").

Among bilingual Hispanic Americans, conversation often drifts easily from Spanish to English and back.

Spanglish is especially handy for discussing new technologies. To say "I am e-mailing," speakers of what is called CyberSpanglish say, "Estoy emaileando." To say "Click the mouse," they do not use *raton*, Spanish for "mouse," but say simply, "Clickea el mouse."

Cuban dialect has been called "Spanish in overdrive." Usage varies too: some Latin Americans say *vos*, others *tú*, to mean a singular, familiar "you."

How many Hispanic Americans are poor?

As of 1994, according to the U.S. Census Bureau, 30.7 percent—nearly a third—of Hispanic Americans lived below the poverty level. That means that a family of four would make under $15,141 per year.

Poverty is more widespread among Hispanic Americans than among white Americans. The proportion of white Americans living under the poverty line was 11.7 percent in 1994. The poverty rate among black Americans was comparable to that among Hispanic Americans: 30.6 percent of blacks lived below the poverty level.

Why are so many Hispanic Americans poor?

Many are recent immigrants from impoverished countries. Many can only find work in unskilled jobs. With effort and education, they or their children may yet achieve middle-class prosperity. Others have been here a long time but suffer from generations of discrimination—notably the Chicanos of the West and Southwest. With poverty come such familiar problems as family instability, drug addiction, and crime. Gangs such as the Latin Kings (founded in the 1940s) seem like routes to status and income for some desperate Hispanic American youths.

Undocumented workers are especially likely to be poor. They often accept low wages and poor working conditions for fear that their employers will turn them in to the INS.

Why do advocates for immigrants prefer to talk about "undocumented workers" rather than "illegal aliens"?

The term "illegal" is loaded with a presumption of criminal guilt. In contrast, "undocumented" is a neutral description of the situation of people who are in the United States without papers proving their legal status. If an immigration court were to hear their cases, it might conceivably uphold their right to be here.

"Illegal alien" is even worse than "illegal immigrant." The term "alien" sounds like a monster from a science fiction movie—like the 1997 movie *Men in Black*, in which the "illegal aliens" were just that.

Is it easy to immigrate legally?

No. Under U.S. immigration laws enacted in 1965 and afterward, no more than 270,000 visas permitting immigration can be issued in any given year. No more than 20,000 visas can be issued to any single country per year. Some categories are exempt from this limitation, such as children of U.S. citizens and political refugees. Even so, the number of visas available is utterly out of proportion to the demand—considering that one million people are caught trying to cross the Mexican border every year.

A preference system governs who will get the coveted immigration visas. Close relatives—children, spouses, parents, siblings—of U.S. citizens and residents are preferred, as are professional and skilled workers. Would-be immigrants may wait years for their turn to come up. Unskilled laborers who are not related to an American have almost no chance at all.

Why do so many people want to crack down on illegal immigrants?

Critics of undocumented immigrants say they take jobs from "real" Americans and burden the welfare system. But supporters say undocumented immigrants take menial, low-paying jobs that Americans would be unlikely to take. Supporters also say that undocumented immigrants are less likely than American citizens to apply for welfare benefits. Why would someone who fears capture and deportation take a chance showing up in a government office?

Despite these arguments, the crackdown has gone on since the 1980s. An immigration act in 1986 offered amnesty (pardon) and legal status to most illegals who had resided in the country continuously since 1982. But it also installed penalties for employers who hire undocumented workers. Another immigration act in 1996 has instituted even tougher measures, including penalties for illegals who try to legalize their status by marrying a U.S. citizen.

A green card is not really green, but pink. This document, which proves that someone is a legal permanent resident of the United States, is commonly known as a green card because it was once aqua-colored.

What are remesas?

These are "remittances"—money that immigrants to the United States send home to their families in Latin America. The immigrants save up the money from their jobs and send it home, often via one of several courier agencies that specialize in the task.

For many Latin American countries, **remesas** are an important source of foreign income, one that goes straight to people who need it. These countries include Mexico, Cuba, the Dominican Republic, and El Salvador. Some of these countries have been vocal in urging the United States not to carry out mass deportations of workers who have entered illegally.

How many American businesses are owned by Hispanic Americans?

Belying the common image of the Hispanic American as a hired hand in someone's factory or field, Latinos are more likely than ever to run their own companies. As of 1992, Hispanic Americans owned 862,605 businesses—5 percent of all the businesses in the country. California, Texas, and Florida have especially high numbers of Hispanic-owned business.

Most Hispanic American businesses are small firms owned by a single proprietor. Many of these firms are new. The number of Hispanic-owned businesses increased 76 percent from 1987 to 1992 —nearly triple the rate of growth for U.S. firms as a whole.

Are the major Spanish-language television networks in the United States owned by Hispanic Americans?

No. Univision and Telemundo are both owned by Anglo companies. (The cable network Galavision is Mexican-owned.) Management and performing talent tend to be white Cubans and South Americans. Mexicans, Puerto Ricans, and Hispanics of mixed race are severely underrepresented.

Many newspapers, magazines, radio stations, and web sites are devoted to Latinos. Some are in Spanish, some in English, some bilingual. The country's best-known Spanish-

A shopper selects a can of Goya beans from supermarket shelves. The Goya company markets an enormous range of products designed to appeal to Hispanics of many different backgrounds.

language newspaper, New York's *El Diario/La Prensa*, is Anglo-owned and has a large proportion of Cubans in its management.

Who founded Goya Foods?

Based in Secaucus, New Jersey, Goya Foods specializes in foods for the U.S. Latino population. It was founded in 1936 by Prudencio Unanue, a Spanish businessman who moved to Puerto Rico before settling in New York. Still headed by a Unanue family member, Goya is now one of the five hundred largest private companies, according to *Forbes* magazine.

Beans and rice are big sellers, but the product line includes everything from fruit nectars to frozen dinners. The company aims to please all Latinos by paying attention to who prefers what. Cubans are more apt to buy long-grain rice, while Puerto Ricans want medium-grain rice. Mexicans like pink beans, Cubans black beans. The company's slogan is familiar to both Anglos and Latinos in many urban areas: "If it's Goya, it has to be good!"

What are those shirts with the two stripes down the front that you often see in Florida?

These cool, comfortable garments are called **guayabera shirts**. They are popular in warm parts of Latin America and among many Hispanic American men—especially in Florida. They have pleated stripes down the front, four pockets, and side vents. No need to tuck them in; they are worn over trousers.

Latinos in Space

The first Latino astronaut was Costa Rican-born Franklin Chang-Diaz (1950–). A physicist who specializes in plasma rockets, he became an astronaut in 1981 and first flew aboard the space shuttle in 1986. California-born physicist Ellen Ochoa (1958–) was the first Latina astronaut. She became an astronaut in 1991 and first flew into space in 1993.

Hispanic Americans have also boldly gone into television space. The starship bridge in the 1990s TV series *Star Trek: Voyager* features two Hispanic Americans: Chicano Robert Beltran as First Officer Chakotay, and Puerto Rican Roxann Biggs-Dawson as Chief Engineer B'Elanna Torres.

Is Andy Garcia Italian?

No, but the actor played Italians in two of his biggest film roles: a rookie G-man in *The Untouchables* (1987) and the heir to a Mafia family in *The Godfather, Part III* (1990). Garcia is a Cuban American. Born in Havana in 1956, he

Astronaut Ellen Ochoa became the first Hispanic American woman in space. She flew as payload commander on the space shuttle *Atlantis* in November 1994. This NASA photo shows her at work in the space shuttle with Mission Commander Donald R. McMonagle.

Actor Andy Garcia appeared as Vincent Mancini in *The Godfather, Part III*. Born in Cuba, Garcia has shone as an Italian American in several Hollywood roles.

fled with his family to Miami after Fidel Castro took power in 1959.

Garcia is one of several Latino actors who have performed in Hollywood films of recent years. Puerto Rican-born Raul Julia, who died in 1994, starred in such films as *Kiss of the Spider Woman* (1985) and *The Addams Family* (1991). Other Hispanic American actors include John Leguizamo, Jimmy Smits, the Sheen-Estevez clan (see the chapter Coming from Spain), and Edward James Olmos (see the chapter Coming from Mexico).

What kind of a background did Rosie Perez come from?

The Puerto Rican actress, born circa 1968, grew up in troubled circumstances in Brooklyn. At twelve, she was put in a group home for cutting a woman's neck. Moving to Los Angeles, she found a constructive way to channel her

Pseudo-Hispanics

Hollywood has a long tradition of using non-Hispanics to play Hispanic roles. Silent-screen "Latin" lover Rudolph Valentino was Italian. Tyrone Power practically made a living playing suave Spaniards in films such as *The Mark of Zorro* (1940).

Blond, blue-eyed Charlton Heston played a Mexican detective in *Touch of Evil* (1958). Things hadn't changed that much by the 1990s. In 1997, Italian Americans Al Pacino and Madonna starred as Latinos in, respectively, *Carlito's Way* and *Evita*.

frenetic energy: as a star of such movies as *Do the Right Thing* (1989) and *White Men Can't Jump* (1992).

Hollywood is becoming an increasingly friendly place for Latina actresses, including Cameron Diaz, Jennifer Lopez,

Rita Hayworth appeared in numerous films throughout the 1940s and 1950s, but few moviegoers knew she was a Hispanic American. Here she is seen with comedian Phil Silvers, center, and dancer Gene Kelly in the 1944 musical *Cover Girl.*

The Hidden Hispanic

Latino performers were rare in the 1930s and '40s, the Golden Era of Hollywood. Mexican-born Lupe Velez was popular for her "Mexican Spitfire" comedies. Dominican American Maria Montez appeared in adventure films. Mexican American Anthony Quinn played minor villains until the 1950s, when he became a full-fledged star.

The greatest exception was the sex goddess Rita Hayworth—and her ethnic origins were all but invisible. Born in Brooklyn in 1918 as Margarita Carmen Cansino, she was the daughter of Spanish-born dancer Eduardo Cansino. She made her first films in 1935 as Rita Cansino, but got little attention until she dyed her black hair auburn and changed her name to the Anglo-sounding Hayworth.

In the 1940s, her career took off. Audiences found Hayworth a beautiful and exciting star in such films as Cover Girl (1944) and Gilda (1946). Soldiers in World War II treasured her pinup picture. Most fans didn't realize she was Latina— even though she had played a Spanish temptress in the bullfighting movie Blood and Sand (1941).

Salma Hayek, and Elizabeth Peña. But Hispanic American actors and actresses regularly confront stereotyping. Latino actors like Andy Garcia and John Leguizamo are often cast as gangsters. As for actresses, Peña says: "I'm usually offered the roles of the prostitute, the mother with seventeen children, or the screaming wife getting beaten up."

What Spanish-speaking country does the samba come from?

None of them. The dance called the **samba** comes from Portuguese-speaking Brazil, where it evolved as a folk dance among people of African descent. It became a dance for urban Brazilian couples in the late nineteenth century, and became internationally popular in the 1920s and 1930s. It was later combined with **bossa nova** music, which is also a Brazilian invention.

Most Latin dances did originate in Spanish-speaking countries. Some have been mentioned in other chapters: salsa, rumba, merengue, cumbia, tango. Other Latin dance crazes have included the **mambo**, **cha-cha**, and **conga** line.

One of the most recent Latin dance crazes in the United States was the macarena. Imported from Spain in the 1990s, it was briefly danced everywhere from weddings to baseball games.

People in the United States discovered Latin American dances in the 1940s and have never stopped enjoying them. Latin rhythm, with its blending of African, Spanish, and Native American traditions, has influenced many forms of music, including jazz and rock. The Latin music industry has greatly expanded in the 1980s and 1990s.

What nationality is Julio Iglesias?

The singer (born in 1943) is from Spain, but he is highly popular throughout Latin America and among Hispanic Americans. His early albums were all in Spanish, but he has recorded songs in other languages as well, including English and French. That practice has made him an international star, appreciated by people of many countries. His Spanish albums include *Emociones*; his English albums include *1100 Bel Air Place*.

Is hammock a Spanish word?

A **hammock** is a bed of netting or canvas that hangs between trees or other supports. The Spanish picked up both the item and the word, *hamaca,* from the Arawak or Taino of the West Indies. Hammocks are now familiar all over the world, particulary in tropical vacation spots and sunny backyards, but are especially popular among Latinos. A hammock is a nice place to take a **siesta,** or afternoon break—a time-honored custom in Latin America.

Where did the card game canasta originate?

This variation on rummy originated in Uruguay and Argentina in the 1940s. With a name that means "basket" in Spanish, **canasta** quickly spread throughout Latin America. It became a big fad in the United States between 1949 and 1951. Its variants include other games with Latino-flavored names, such as Bolivia, Uruguay, and Samba.

Who was the first Latino to break into major league baseball?

It was Esteban Bellan in 1871. But Hispanics did not become a major force in baseball until after 1947, when Jackie Robinson made it possible for players to be non-white. Since then, people from many parts of Latin America have come to make up a large percentage of many U.S. baseball teams. Besides Roberto Clemente (see the chapter Coming from Puerto Rico) and others previously mentioned, their numbers have included Roberto and Sandy Alomar, Bobby Avila, Bobby Bonilla, José Canseco, Orlando Cepada, Willie Hernandez, Jesse Orosco, Tony Perez, Ruben Sierra, Joe Torre, and Fernando Valenzuela.

Who was the first Puerto Rican to break into professional golf?

It was Juan "Chi Chi" Rodriguez. Born in Puerto Rico in 1937, he worked as a caddy at age six. Too poor to afford to buy equipment, he made his own golf club from a guava tree branch and practiced his swing on tin cans. By the 1960s, his talent had taken him to the top ten of the professional golf circuit.

Soccer, known as football outside North America, has become increasingly popular in the United States, due in part to the enthusiasm of Hispanic fans. Here, the Argentinian and Chilean teams face each other in Santiago, Chile, in a 1997 match to help determine who goes to the France 1998 World Cup. Argentina won, 2-1.

Odd Jobs

Hispanic Americans do all kinds of work. Here is an assortment of occupations that some have pursued. You may be surprised to hear that some on the list are Latino.

Lyle Alzado: Football lineman

Martina Arroyo: Opera singer and sometime guest star on TV's *The Odd Couple*

Joan Baez: Folksinger

Jerry Garcia: Deceased leader of the Grateful Dead

Richard "Cheech" Marin: Film and TV actor, formerly of the comedy duo Cheech and Chong

Antonia Novello: First female and first Hispanic American U.S. surgeon general (under President George Bush)

Geraldo Rivera: Occasionally rowdy talk show host and TV journalist

Paul Rodriguez: Stand-up comedian and actor

Jon Secada: Singer and heartthrob

Christy Turlington: Supermodel, notably in Calvin Klein ads

Vanna White: Letter turner on the TV game show *Wheel of Fortune*

Another pioneer among Latino golfers was Lee Trevino, a Mexican American born in Dallas in 1939. He also started playing professionally in the 1960s.

What kind of game is fútbol?

This is the Latin American name for soccer, one of the region's favorite sports. Another favorite pastime is *béisbol,* or baseball. American football has not really caught on in Latin America. But tennis, golf, and boxing have long been crowd-pleasers.

GLOSSARY

A
amigo a friend
Anglo a white, English-speaking American who is not Hispanic
arrastra pulverizing tool used in extracting gold from rocks
arroz moro Cuban dish of beans and rice
asopao a chicken-and-rice dish
atrevimiento daring, boldness

B
bandido a bandit
barbacoa a meal of lamb or goat cooked whole in a heated pit
barrio a neighborhood in which Hispanic Americans live; from Spanish for
    "neighborhood"
batea flat-bottomed pan used in mining gold from streams and rivers
batido a tropical milkshake
blanco a white person
bodega a small, family-owned grocery store
bongo tube drum played by beating with the hands
boniato a sweet potato, often served stuffed and deep-fried
bossa nova Brazilian musical form
botánica a store that sells religious paraphernalia, including charms, incense, and
    herbs
bracero from the 1940s to the 1960s, a Mexican laborer temporarily admitted to the
    United States to work
buckaroo a cowboy; from Spanish vaquero
burrito a soft flour tortilla wrapped around meat, beans, or cheese

C
cafecita Cuban espresso in a small cup; also called cafe cubano, or Cuban coffee
Californio Californian of Mexican descent, particularly before the United States
    takeover in 1848
canasta card game originating in Latin America; from Spanish for "basket"
caramba expression of surprise or annoyance
caudillo chief; a dictator who rules a country by military force
cha-cha a fast dance
Chicano (male) or **Chicana** (female) a Mexican American
chili con carne a dish that combines chili peppers, meat (carne), beans, and spices
colonia a colony or temporary settlement of Mexican Americans

comidas criollas Caribbean or Creole food

compadrazgo the system by which a compadre, or coparent, is selected to watch over a child

compadre a coparent, or one who watches over a friend's child, especially a godfather or godmother; also a term for a pal or comrade

condor a vulture found in the Andes and California

contra rebel against the left-wing government of Nicaragua during the 1980s

converso in fifteenth-century Spain, a Jew who converted to Christianity

costeño a person from northern coastal Colombia who combines African, Spanish, and Native American ancestry

coyote a smuggler of undocumented immigrants from Mexico

Creole 1. a person of pure European descent born in Spanish America or the West Indies; 2. native to the West Indies; 3. a person of mixed African and European ancestry who speaks creole, a pidgin language blending two or more other languages

criollo Creole

cuchifritos fried pork entrails

cumbia Colombian dance and musical form

curandera a folk healer, particularly among Mexican Americans

D

danza El Salvadoran dance

death squad paramilitary group that kidnaps, tortures, and murders people for their political views; often allied to a government

de color a person "of color"; one with dark-brown skin

desperado a criminal, from Spanish *desesperado*, "desperate man"

disappear in reference to political oppression: to be abducted for one's political views, with the presumption that the abducted person will be imprisoned or murdered

E

enchilada a soft flour tortilla wrapped around meat and cheese and served with a topping of tomato-chili sauce

encomienda land grant in Spain's American colonies

F

fajita marinated, grilled meat served in a tortilla

fiesta a party, celebration, or religious feast day

flamenco Spanish dance and musical form

flan a custard dessert

fútbol soccer

G

gringo derogatory term for a person from a non–Spanish-speaking country, particularly an English-speaking person

guayabera a shirt with pleated stripes down the front and vents on the sides

guiro a scraper (musical instrument)

gusano derogatory Cuban term for Cuban exiles; from Spanish for "worm"

H
hammock a bed of netting or canvas suspended between supports

hasta la vista good-bye

Hispanic a person whose ancestors came from Spain or from one of the world's Spanish-speaking cultures

Hispanic American a Hispanic who is a citizen or resident of the United States

hispano a Hispanic or Spanish person; also, a New Mexican who claims descent from the region's original Spanish settlers

hombre a man

I
independentista political activist who demands independence, especially for Puerto Rico

indio an American Indian, or one who looks like an American Indian

J
jai alai Basque game played with a ball and wicker baskets attached to players' arms

jefe a chief

jíbaro a Puerto Rican term for farm worker

junta a small group of military officers sharing joint rule over a country

L
Ladino 1. in Central America, a person of mixed European and Native American origin, or a Native American who has adopted Spanish language and culture; 2. the language spoken by Sephardic Jews

Latin America the parts of the Americas south of the mainland United States in which the dominant languages are Spanish, Portuguese, or French

Latino (male) or **Latina** (female) a Latin American or Hispanic

lechón roast suckling pig

M
machismo the quality of maleness, including such aspects as courage, honor, virility, and toughness

macho male; exhibiting qualities such as courage, honor, virility, and toughness

madrina a godmother

mambo Latin dance

maraca a hollow rhythm instrument filled with seeds or pebbles, held in the hand and shaken

mariachi band a strolling Mexican band that plays guitars, violins, and trumpets

Marielito one of a group of Cuban refugees who came to the United States in the Mariel boatlift of 1980

marimba a large, wooden percussion instrument

marqueta a market

merengue Dominican dance and musical form

mestizo a person of mixed European and Native American ancestry

mofongo a dish combining plantains, beans, and pork

mole poblano a sauce combining chili peppers, garlic, bananas, onions, and unsweetened chocolate

moreno a black person

Moros y Christianos "Moors and Christians," a dish of beans and rice
mulatto a person of mixed European and African ancestry
mutualista a Mexican American mutual aid society

N

negro or **negrito** a black person or little black person; used by some Latinos as terms of endearment
Neorican *see* Nuyorican
nueva canción song movement emphasizing social protest; from Spanish for "new song"
Nuyorican a Puerto Rican New Yorker

O

orishá a spirit or god in Santería; a santo

P

padrino a godfather
pahry Puerto Rican term for party
pampa prairie
partera a midwife; a person assisting at childbirth
pasteles boiled pies
pava a traditional Puerto Rican straw hat
piñata a decorated container full of candy and toys, to be broken by children at parties
plantain a cooking banana
pocho derogatory term used by people in Mexico to describe a Mexican American; also, a term of endearment meaning "little one"
poncho a blanketlike cloak with a hole in the center for the head
posada a Mexican American Christmas pageant commemorating the efforts of the Virgin Mary and Joseph to find an inn on Christmas Eve
presidio a fort built by the Spanish in the colonial Americas
pueblo a village
Pueblo Native American people of the southwestern United States who lived in villages before the Spanish arrived

Q

quince a party held to celebrate a Cuban girl's fifteenth birthday

R

remesa remittance; money that a Hispanic American sends home to his or her family in Latin America
ropa vieja Cuban stew of shredded beef
rumba Cuban dance and musical form

S

salsa dance music that blends the Afro-Caribbean traditions of Puerto Rico and Cuba with American jazz
samba Brazilian dance
Santería a religion of Cuba, Puerto Rico, and elsewhere in Latin America that blends Roman Catholicism and African Yoruba religion

santo a saint; in Santería, a saint who is also a deity of Africa's Yoruba religion

Sephardic Jew a believer in Judaism who lived in Spain and Portugal before the sixteenth century, or a descendant of such Jews

siesta an afternoon nap

sofrito a Puerto Rican seasoning paste

sombrero a hat

spic derogatory term for a Hispanic

strongman a dictator who rules by military force

T

taco a hard corn tortilla folded around ground meat, beans, or cheese

tamale fried, chopped meat and crushed peppers that have been rolled in cornmeal dough, wrapped in corn husks, and steamed

tambora a barrel drum

tango Argentinian dance and musical form

Tejano a Texan who is a Mexican American

Tex-Mex blending elements from Mexico and the southwestern United States (especially Texas), as in music or food

tortilla a flat, round bread, like a pancake, made from cornmeal or wheat flour and baked on a hot surface

trigueño a dark or swarthy person; among Puerto Ricans, a person with light brown skin, as opposed to someone *de color* (of color), with dark brown skin

V

vallenato Colombian musical ensemble, usually including a diatonic button accordion, drums, shakers, and scrapers

W

wetback derogatory term for a Mexican American

Y

yuca a starchy root vegetable

YUCA Young, Upwardly Mobile Cuban American

Z

zoot suit a suit with exaggerated styling, including a long coat and baggy pants, worn by urban youths in the 1940s

SELECTED BIBLIOGRAPHY

Acuña, Rodolfo. *Occupied America: A History of Chicanos*, 2nd ed. New York: Harper & Row, 1981.

Aliotta, Jerome J. *The Puerto Ricans*. New York: Chelsea House, 1991.

Atkin, S. Beth. *Voices from the Fields: Children of Migrant Farmworkers Tell Their Stories*. Boston: Little, Brown, 1993.

Bachelis, Faren. *The Central Americans*. New York: Chelsea House, 1990.

Bernardo, Stephanie. *The Ethnic Almanac*. Garden City, N.Y.: Dolphin, 1981.

Chernow, Barbara A., and George A. Vallasi. *The Columbia Encyclopedia*. 5th ed. New York: Columbia University Press, 1993.

Corey, Melinda, and George Ochoa. *American History: The New York Public Library Book of Answers*. New York: Fireside, 1993.

Cullison, Alan. *The South Americans*. New York: Chelsea House, 1991.

Davis, Kenneth C. *Don't Know Much About History*. New York: Avon, 1990.

Dwyer, Christopher. *The Dominican Americans*. New York: Chelsea House, 1991.

ElPuebloNet (web site). Latino Cultures & History Forum: http://www.ma.iup.edu/Pueblo/ElPuebloNet.html.

Fernández-Shaw, Carlos M. *The Hispanic Presence in North America: From 1492 to Today*. Translation by Alfonso Bertodano Stourton, et al. New York: Facts On File, 1991.

Garver, Susan, and Paula McGuire. *Coming to North America: From Mexico, Cuba, and Puerto Rico*. New York: Delacorte, 1981.

Gernand, Renèe. *The Cuban Americans*. New York: Chelsea House, 1988.

Hardy, Phil, and Dave Laing. *The Faber Companion to 20th-Century Popular Music*. London: Faber & Faber, 1990.

Johnson, Otto, ed. *Information Please Almanac 1997.* 50th ed. Boston: Houghton Mifflin, 1997.

Katz, Ephraim. *The Film Encyclopedia.* 2nd ed. New York: HarperPerennial, 1994.

La Raza Online (web site). http://www.laraza.com.

Lannert, Paula. *Mexican Americans.* Vero Beach, Fla.: Rourke Corp., 1991.

LatinoLink (web site). http://www.latinolink.com.

Lick, Sue Fagalde. *The Iberian Americans.* New York: Chelsea House, 1990.

Meier, Matt S., and Feliciano Ribera. *Mexican Americans/American Mexicans: From Conquistadors to Chicanos.* New York: Hill & Wang, 1993.

Meltzer, Milton. *The Hispanic-Americans.* New York: Thomas Y. Crowell, 1982.

Microsoft Encarta 97 Encyclopedia. Microsoft, 1993–1996.

Morison, Samuel Eliot. *The European Discovery of America: The Southern Voyages, A.D. 1492–1616.* New York: Oxford University Press, 1974.

———. *The Oxford History of the American People.* New York: New American Library, 1972.

Novas, Himilce. *Everything You Need to Know About Latino History.* New York: Plume, 1994.

Ochoa, George. *The Fall of Mexico City.* Englewood Cliffs, N.J.: Silver Burdett, 1989.

Rodríguez, Clara E. *Puerto Ricans: Born in the U.S.A.* Boston: Unwin Hyman, 1989.

Shorris, Earl. *Latinos: A Biography of the People.* New York: W. W. Norton, 1992.

Stavans, Ilan. *The Hispanic Condition: Reflections on Culture and Identity in America.* New York: HarperCollins, 1995.

Things Latino at EgoWeb—Connections to CyberRaza (web site). http://www.egoiste.edb.utexas.edu/html/latinos.html.

Zinn, Howard. *A People's History of the United States.* New York: Harper & Row, 1980.

THE NEW YORK PUBLIC LIBRARY'S RECOMMENDED READING LIST

Latinas!: Women of Achievement. Detroit, MI: Visible Ink Press, 1996.

Aliotta, Jerome J. *The Puerto Ricans.* New York: Chelsea House, 1996.

Bachrach, Deborah. *The Spanish-American War.* San Diego, CA: Lucent Books, 1991.

Bandon, Alexandra. *Dominican Americans.* Parsippany, NJ: New Discovery Books, 1995.

Bernier-Grand, Carmen T. *Poet and Politician of Puerto Rico: Don Luis Munoz Marin.* New York: Orchard Books, 1995.

Byers, Ann. *Jaime Escalante: Sensational Teacher.* Springfield, NJ: Enslow Publishers, 1996.

Catalano, Grace. *Gloria Estefan.* New York: St. Martin's Press, 1991.

Cockcroft, James D. *Latinos in the Making of the United States.* New York: Franklin Watts, 1995.

Dolan, Sean. *Junipero Serra.* New York: Chelsea House, 1991.

Garcia, John A. *The Success of Hispanic Magazine.* New York: Walker and Co., 1996.

Garza, Hedda. *Joan Baez.* New York: Chelsea House, 1991.

Gonzales, Doreen. *Cesar Chavez: Leader for Migrant Farm Workers.* Springfield, NJ: Enslow Publishers, 1996.

Harlan, Judith. *Hispanic American Voters: A Voice in American Politics.* New York: Franklin Watts, 1988.

Hoobler, Dorothy and Thomas Hoobler. *The Cuban American Family Album.* New York: Oxford University Press, 1996.

———. *The Mexican American Family Album.* New York: Oxford University Press, 1994.

Kanellos, Nicolas. *Hispanic Firsts: 500 Years of Extraordinary Achievement*. Detroit, MI: Gale, 1997.

Lankford, Mary D. Quinceanera: *A Latina's Journey to Womanhood*. Brookfield, CT: Millbrook Press, 1994.

Marton, Betty A. *Ruben Blades*. New York: Chelsea House, 1992.

Morey, Janet. *Famous Hispanic Americans*. New York: Cobblehill Books, 1996.

Nardo, Don. *The Mexican-American War*. San Diego, CA: Lucent Books, 1991.

Novas, Himilce. *Everything You Need to Know About Latino History*. New York: Penguin, 1994.

Palacios, Argentina. *Standing Tall: The Stories of Ten Hispanic Americans*. New York: Scholastic, 1994.

Press, Skip. *Charlie Sheen, Emilio Estevez and Martin Sheen*. Parsippany, NJ: Crestwood House, 1996.

Sinnott, Susan. *Extraordinary Hispanic Americans*. Chicago: Childrens Press, 1991.

Stefoff, Rebecca. *Raul Julia*. New York: Chelsea House, 1994.

Suntree, Susan. *Rita Moreno*. New York: Chelsea House, 1993.

Walker, Paul Robert. *Pride of Puerto Rico: The Life of Roberto Clemente*. San Diego, CA: Harcourt Brace Jovanovich, 1988.

Wolf, Bernard. *In This Proud Land: The Story of a Mexican American Family*. Philadelphia: Lippincott, 1978.

INDEX

Note: Page numbers in italics indicate illustrations.

Photography Credits

p. 10, The Map Division of the New York Public Library, Astor, Lenox, and Tilden Foundations; p. 16, Ullman/MONKMEYER; p. 21, Office of Special Collections, The Picture Collection of the New York Public Library, Astor, Lenox, and Tilden Foundations; p. 27, Neg. No.: 315090, Photo: Rice and Bierwent, Courtesy Department of Library Services, American Museum of Natural History; pp. 32, 40, Library of Congress; p. 42, Corbis-Bettmann; p. 44, Corbis; pp. 52, 53, Library of Congress; p. 55, 62, Corbis-Bettmann; pp. 65, 68, Library of Congress; p. 72, UPI/Corbis-Bettmann; p. 79, Montaine/MONKMEYER; p. 85, Library of Congress; p. 90, UPI/Corbis-Bettmann; p. 96, Courtesy Fernando Ferrer; p. 102, Library of Congress; p. 109, Photo Number ST 19-4-62, Courtesy John F. Kennedy Library; p. 120, UPI/Corbis-Bettmann; p. 123, Courtesy Oscar de la Renta; p. 124, UPI/Corbis-Bettmann; p. 126, The Map Division of the New York Public Library, Astor, Lenox, and Tilden Foundations; pp. 127, 128, Library of Congress; p. 132, Reuters/Corbis-Bettmann; p. 138, Photofest; p. 141, The Map Division of the New York Public Library, Astor, Lenox, and Tilden Foundations; p. 143, UPI/Corbis-Bettmann; p. 154, The Northeastern Nevada Museum, Elko, Nevada; p. 155, Courtesy Florida Gaming Commission; p. 157, Photofest; p. 169, Collins/MONKMEYER; p. 170, Courtesy National Aeronautics and Space Administration; pp. 171, 172, Photofest; p. 175, Agence France Presse/Corbis-Bettmann.